WISDOM
CALLS
The Moral Story of the Hebrew Bible

Paul Lewis

© 2017

Published in the United States by Nurturing Faith Inc., Macon GA,

www.nurturingfaith.net.

Library of Congress Cataloging-in-Publication Data is available.

ISBN 978-1-63528-009-8

All quotations from the Hebrew Bible in this book come from the
Tanakh translation of the Jewish Publication Society, in the *Jewish Study Bible*
(New York: Oxford University Press), 2004.

For Marsha and Timothy

Experience as both professor and pastor confirms that many Christians who take faith seriously yearn for ways to inhabit the Old Testament text and embrace it as a living organism. They ask, "How can I engage the Hebrew Bible in ways that simultaneously honor its integrity and display its functional benefit for living intentionally in complex, and sometimes disordered, times? How can the Old Testament be a resource for my development as a moral person?" In this highly suggestive and even sometimes edgy book, Paul Lewis has undertaken a novel approach for discerning how both Jews and Christians can learn about how their development as moral and wise persons are displayed in the Hebrew Bible.

—The Rev. Dr. Harmon Smith,
Emeritus Professor of Moral Theology (Divinity) and
Emeritus Professor of Community and Family Medicine (Medicine)
at Duke University

Paul Lewis is scholarly, spiritual and...well...worldly—in the best sense of the word. So, whether you wander the halls of academia, regularly sit in a church, or just hang out in coffee shops, his humor, heart, and insight will delight and benefit you. Paul shares a refreshing view of biblical literature that guides us past both the rigidity of legalistic answers and the murky, mysterious unanswerable questions of faith to a space of mature thought for our messy worlds. I'm guessing you'll finish this book and think, "My bible, my life and my world make a little more sense to me now."

—Dr. Jim Dant,
Pastor, First Baptist Greenville,
Greenville, South Carolina

Paul Lewis gifts the reader with a path into the Old Testament that integrates religious and psychological frameworks. The book is engagingly written and entices the reader to move forward on the path to wisdom. We can all benefit from such assistance!

—Dr. Darcia Narvaez,
Professor of Psychology, University of Notre Dame

In this perceptive and noteworthy work, Paul Lewis applies criterion generally associated with wisdom literature to the entirety of the Hebrew Scriptures, creating a very fresh focus that amplifies our understanding of these sacred texts.

—Rabbi Larry Schlesinger,
Temple Beth Israel, Macon, Georgia

Contents

PREFACE

"And Now for Something Completely Different!"

That phrase, the opening line for each episode of the groundbreaking British comedy series *Monty Python's Flying Circus*, might well describe this book, for it is *not* a standard introduction to the Old Testament. This book should be treated instead as a thought experiment that investigates the question, "What does the Old Testament teach us about moral development?" The answer that I will develop over the course of the book is that it calls us to develop wisdom to live in a complex world full of competing voices. This is, in short, what I am calling the moral story of the Hebrew Bible. In fact, I will go further to suggest that reading the Old Testament as Hebrew Bible actually initiates its readers into a process of moral development, the end point of which is wisdom.

Given the eccentricities of this work, readers can—and should—ask, "How did you come up with this project?" Three primary factors led me down this path. First, I have long been intrigued by Jack Miles' Pulitzer Prize-winning work *God: a Biography*.[1] A Jesuit-trained literary critic, Miles engages in his own thought experiment by reading the Old Testament in Hebrew Bible order as a continuous narrative. (See the next chapter for an explanation of the difference between the two.) More than that, Miles reads the story with one question in mind: "What happens to God as a character in the story?" The result is an intriguing view of God. In this book, we will take a similar approach as Miles, but will ask a different question, since I am not a literary critic. I am instead a Christian ethicist who is interested in moral development and who teaches multiple sections of Old Testament each year at a private university. So I must confess that, to paraphrase the old television commercial, "I am not an Old Testament scholar, but I play one in the classroom."

Second, a few years ago, I was looking for a way of "aligning" (a current buzzword) my teaching obligations with my research interests so that I could work more "efficiently" (yet another bit of jargon these days that is often an excuse for requiring people to do more with less. Leaders demanding such should read Exodus and see how well that turned out for Pharaoh. But I digress.) Doing some research on the Bible and character development, I discovered an essay by Old Testament scholar William P. Brown, who argues that the structure of the book of Proverbs moves readers from simplistic reliance on rules as the basis of morality to union with wisdom. Brown demonstrates how the opening poem and different collections of proverbs that make up the book lead the reader into increasing moral complexity as later sections critique overly simplistic views found earlier in the book. As he puts it, "In short, the bookends of Proverbs trace the formation of moral character that culminates in the union of Wisdom and her student, a movement that spans the process of maturation from receptive child to responsible adult, from dependent to patriarch."[2] This line of thought was one that I believed could fruitfully be applied to the Hebrew Scriptures as a whole—a task I have undertaken in this work.

A third factor in the genesis of this project is my interest in moral development, an interest that goes back to my days as a psychology major in college. At that time, Lawrence Kohlberg's research dominated the topic. Drawing from the cognitive theories of Jean Piaget, Kohlberg identified six stages in the development of moral reasoning clustered into three levels that he called the pre-conventional, conventional, and post-conventional. These levels are distinguished by the basis upon which moral decisions are made. In pre-conventional reasoning, moral decisions are based on the impact they will have on the self—we decide on the basis of whether we will benefit or not. In conventional moral reasoning, decisions are based on social conventions, or what other people, customs, laws, etc., expect of us. In contrast to these two levels, those who reason at the post-conventional level base their decisions on so-called "transcendent ideals," such as human rights or justice.

A number of critics have pointed out legitimate problems with Kohl-berg's theory, but two features of his work are important for our pur-poses. The first is that we can and do develop morally over our lifespan. The second is that the direction of development goes from a focus on self to a focus on laws to a focus on principles. My question (and that of Kohlberg's critics, as we will see in the appendix to this book) is, "Is this enough?" Based on my reading of the Hebrew Bible, my answer is, "No." Reading the Old Testament as Hebrew Bible invites us to develop morally by moving from a focus on self to law and then to principles, but then compels us to go beyond in a quest for wisdom.

All of this is to say, again, that this book is not another introduction to the Old Testament—we have too many good ones already (some of which are overpriced, by the way). Neither is this book a study in con-temporary moral psychology. Instead it is an attempt to integrate disci-plines in a way that respects the scholarship of both fields but is slavishly beholden to neither. The result, for me at least, is a provocative and fruit-ful way of reading these ancient texts that helps us see their contemporary relevance—and hopefully challenges us to become wiser.

Even though this book is not another standard textbook, I do think it is best read in combination with a good study Bible and perhaps a more traditional introduction. For study Bibles, I recommend the *Jewish Study Bible* (now in a second edition), not only because the books occur in the order of the Hebrew Scriptures rather than the Christian Old Testament, but because the notes and articles add interesting material on Judaism's use and understanding of these texts. All of this helps us read these texts again, as if for the first time (with apologies to Marcus Borg's *Reading the Bible Again for the First Time*, which is also a good introduction to the Bible as a whole). I also recommend *The Meaning of the Bible: What the Jewish Scriptures and Christian Old Testament Can Teach Us*, by Douglas A. Knight and Amy-Jill Levine. Knight is Christian and Levine is Jewish, and together they have put together a wonderful synthesis of the scholar-ship of both traditions. For standard introductions to the Old Testament, see the recommended readings at the end of the book.

Although I am a college teacher, I do not write with an exclusively undergraduate audience in mind. I write as well for people who want to

think about their faith and who are open to reading these texts in fresh
ways. The goal of doing this is not to be novel for the sake of being novel, but to gain insights that we otherwise miss because we all too often
take these texts for granted. Thus I hope that this book will be useful to
study groups in different religious communities, along with undergraduate classrooms.

Before saying more about the project, I must first pause to acknowledge groups and individuals who have contributed to this work by allowing me to try out these ideas in various settings: the Hailey Sunday
School Class at Highland Hills Baptist Church in Macon, Ga.; the Seek-
ers Sunday School Class at First Baptist Church of Christ in Macon,
Ga.; students in my sections of Old Testament at Mercer University in
the spring semesters of 2014 and 2016; participants in the "Virtue and
Its Development" conference held at the University of Notre Dame in
May 2014; and the conference "Between the Disciplines: from Theory
to Practice," held at Mercer University in March 2015. Individuals who
have read and commented on this material at various stages of development and who have offered valuable (and sometimes blunt) commen-
tary include Jim Dant, Pastor of First Baptist Church in Greenville, S.C.;
Janell Johnson, a colleague at Mercer—and a bona fide Old Testament
scholar; Amy-Jill Levine, Professor of New Testament and Jewish Studies at Vanderbilt University; Darcia Narvaez, Professor of Psychology at
the University of Notre Dame; and Rabbi Larry Schlesinger, now retired
from Temple Beth Israel in Macon, Ga. I am grateful, too, to David Cas-
sady, John Peirce, Lex Horton, and others at Nurturing Faith who were
willing to take a risk on this project, one that some readers will at times
find shocking, irreverent, and/or simply weird.

I must also express my gratitude for the financial support that made
the research and publication of this book possible. Richard F. Wilson,
Chair of the Roberts Department of Religion at Mercer, has been gen-
erous over the past few years with funds from the department's Edward
Dargan Johnston fund for research. All of us in the department are in-
debted to Dr. Johnston's generosity and foresight in establishing this fund.
Wayne C. Glasgow, Senior Vice Provost for Research at Mercer, has also
generously supported this work, as has Highland Hills Baptist Church.

Last, but certainly not least, I dedicate this book to my wife and son. Although they are not God, they do serve as God's servants by drawing me out of myself into the service of a wider good.

I conclude with a preview of what is to come. Chapter One will explain in more detail how I want readers to enter into these texts. The next three chapters will be built around the three-part structure of the Hebrew Bible. Chapter Two will therefore explore what snapshots from the Law tell us about moral development. Chapter Three will do the same for the Prophets. Chapter Four will immerse us in the conflicts and complexities found in selections from the Writings. Chapter Five will put wisdom on center stage as we explore what wisdom meant in the ancient world and engage in some exercises intended to help us more consciously and conscientiously deal wisely with diversity. Each chapter will contain questions for discussion. An appendix will review the psychological literature that has informed this study. A bibliography and recommendations for further reading can be found at the end of the book.

I hope that readers will find that this book is more than an eccentric and illuminating way of reading the Old Testament. I hope that they will also read it as an invitation to do today what the biblical writers did in their day, namely discern what it means, in practice, to live wisely as the faithful people of God. Our world, as polarized as it is politically and religiously, is surely as contentious as that faced by the ancient Jewish people after the Exile. Perhaps we can learn from them as we try to negotiate gracefully the conflicting voices heard in our so-called "culture wars."

Endnotes

[1] New York: Vintage Books, 1995.

[2] See his "The Pedagogy of Proverbs 10:1-31:9," in *Character and Scripture: Moral Formation, Community, and Biblical Interpretation*, edited by William P. Brown (Grand Rapids: William B. Eerdmans Publishing Company, 2002), 153.

CHAPTER ONE

An Experiment in Reading the Old Testament

The Need for Wisdom Now—and Then

As any pollster knows, how we ask a question will shape the answer we get. So, for example, if we read the Bible asking how a text might inspire us, we will get a different answer than if we ask how an author characterizes a person in the story. These questions do not necessarily lead to mutually exclusive answers, of course, for we might find ourselves inspired by examining how the authors characterize Abraham in the narratives of Genesis. Nonetheless, we get different answers because we have asked different questions—and in this book we will be asking a question about moral development.

As I said in the Preface, readers should treat this book as a thought experiment that investigates the question, "What can we learn from the Hebrew Bible about moral development?" Whether we agree or not on the legitimacy of this way of reading the Bible, I suspect we might be able to agree that wisdom is a quality that is needed today as much as any other era, if not more so. In our so-called information age, where information is only a few seconds away thanks to Google and the Internet, we easily become inundated with data. But we have a hard time knowing whether the information we find is accurate and an even harder time knowing how to put it to use for good purposes.

Not only are we inundated with information, but we also live in an increasingly contentious and uncivil age. Political partisanship makes it harder to work together for a common good. To be elected, candidates increasingly play to selected groups of voters, regardless of what their own personal views might be. This political theater not only leads voters to be suspicious of a candidate's sincerity but also to gridlock, as fewer people are willing to make the compromises necessary to pass legislation. Of course, the problem is not just a matter of politics, for communities of faith are increasingly divided into groups whose posturing on all sides of an issue is all too strident. The easy access to social media gives ready-made platforms to Christians who, for example, are both for and against gay marriage. It takes wisdom to discern who, if anyone, is "right" on any contentious issue. As we will see, the days in which the ancient Jewish people collected these texts into canon are in interesting ways somewhat like ours, for theirs was a world in which many different voices vied for attention.

A major difference between that world and ours, however, is that in ancient days wisdom was understood to be, if not *the* most important virtue or character trait one could have, at least a very important one. For the ancients, wisdom meant, at least in part, the ability to discern the course of action that would achieve the most of what is considered "the good" as is possible in a particular set of circumstances.[1] Wisdom thus presupposed a vision of the good that people tried to actualize within the limits and possibilities of their circumstances. The importance of wisdom continued to be recognized through the Middle Ages, but then became marginalized in the modern era as people became enthralled with scientific and technical rationality. It is only after World War II—when we have seen the destructive power of scientific and technical rationality in the form of nuclear weapons and the Holocaust—that more and more people have come to see the need for wisdom; that is, for putting knowledge once again into the service of the good. The Human Genome Project, the massive effort of the late 1990s to decode the human genome, serves as an example. Investigators had the foresight to devote 5 percent of the project's multimillion-dollar budget to exploring the moral implications of their research. Hopefully, their foresight signifies that we are coming full circle to a renewed appreciation for wisdom. If so, then the thought experiment of this book is a timely one.

Since this book is a thought experiment and scientific literature usually includes a discussion of the method used in the experiment, the rest of this chapter will set out the method that will guide our exploration. This method first means giving the history behind the texts its due, but no more than its due. Secondly, it means treating these texts as canon, a collection of texts that have come to be recognized by the community of faith as telling a story that we need to hear over and over again if we are to be faithful people of God. Finally, the method asks us to read these canonical texts with fresh eyes, as naïve readers.

Giving History Its Due

The books that comprise the Hebrew Bible were written somewhere between 1000-100 BCE by different authors in different circumstances and can be classified into different literary genres.[2] Moreover, portions of

A Quick Guide to Biblical Genres and "Criticism"

The Hebrew Bible contains many different kinds of literature, including myth, history, prophetic oracle, poetry, wisdom, and apocalyptic. In using these terms for the different literary genres found in the TNK, we should be careful not to read into them our popular ideas of what the term genre means. For example, we tend to equate myths with fairy tales, or stories that are not true, whereas when used to designate ancient literature, the term means roughly a story that communicates truths about life in ways that are not necessarily "factually" true.

Nor should we think that what "history" meant then is what the term means now. Popularly, history means an objective account of what "really" happened. In the ancient world, "histories" were intended to teach a lesson of some sort or another. We might cynically say that histories

deliberately put a spin on accounts of what happened. Of course, we also need to realize, too, that today is not much different. Even what a video camera captures will not give us the full record of events because it cannot capture everything that is going on in a room or a society. Moreover, viewers still have to interpret what they see when watching the recording.

Modern Christian and Jewish scholars have developed a variety of methods for studying these texts that recognize their historical character, literary genre, and editorial history. These include, but are not limited to:

Source Criticism: Seeks to identify the sources that an author or editor used in writing a text. For example, source critics say that the Law is made up of four different literary sources known by the abbreviations J, E, P, and D.

continued on page 4

continued from page 3

Textual Criticism: Seeks to recover the original reading of a text by working through the differences found between the many existing copies of biblical manuscripts.

Form Criticism: Seeks to recover the oral form behind the written text and how that story may have functioned in its original setting.

Redaction Criticism: Seeks to recover the stages by which a text was edited.

Note, too, that the scholars who deveoped modern biblical studies were often German, and so the form of study they developed was often called "___ Geschichte," the German word for history. However, when the work of these scholars was translated into English, it was translated as "___ Criticism," which was a public relations blow to the academic study of the Bible because it made it seem as if these scholars were out to discredit the Bible. Some were, to be sure, but most were people of faith.

the written text reflect much older oral traditions that had been passed down for generations before finally being written. The reality is that we simply do not know as much as we would like to know about the when, where, and why behind specific texts, although we can usually make educated guesses. The same is largely true of the process by which these texts were eventually collected together to form the Hebrew Bible, although we are on a bit firmer ground there.

It is widely accepted that the Hebrew Bible formed in three stages that correspond to its three sections: Torah (Law), Nevi'im (Prophets), and Kethuvim (Writings), the names of which serve as another name for the collection rather than Hebrew Bible: TNK (the term I will use), or *Tanakh*. The first set of literature to be collected was the Law, as is indicated in stories from Ezra and Nehemiah that suggest that after the Exile, Ezra returned from Babylon to Jerusalem with a scroll containing the Torah (see, for example, Nehemiah 8:1-8). That—and the reception and response to reading the Torah—indicates that this section of the Hebrew Bible was first considered sacred text around the year 400 BCE. The next section of the TNK, the Prophets, seems to have achieved similar status around two centuries later, whereas the Writings did not attain canonical status until about 100 CE at the earliest—and perhaps even significantly later.

Regardless of the dates, the event that crystalized and motivated this process of collecting sacred literature is the Babylonian Exile. The Exile refers to the Babylonian captivity of the ancient Jewish people in the 6th century BCE. A (very) brief history is as follows: After the death of King Solomon in 922 BCE, the nation of Israel splits. The ten tribes in the north keep the name Israel and make Samaria their capital. The two tribes in the south take the name Judah and keep Jerusalem as their capital. Unlike the ten northern tribes, they maintain a hereditary monarchy so that their king is always a descendant of David. In 722 BCE, Israel falls to the Assyrian Empire, leaving Judah as the last semi-independent vestige of the once united and thriving Israel. Babylon then displaces Assyria as the dominant empire and eventually invades Judah. In 587 BCE, the Babylonian armies destroy Jerusalem and the Temple there. Not only does this event represent a devastating military victory for the Babylonians but also a dispiriting symbolic victory, for now the symbols of Jewish political power and religious devotion lie in ruins, with the king of Judah, Zedekiah, taken prisoner to Babylon.[3] As to what happens to the population of Judah, the Babylonians take at least the leadership elites into captivity, while others escape as refugees to North Africa and places around the Mediterranean.

While we do not know how many people were actually displaced, the records indicate that the event, understandably enough, was emotionally and theologically traumatic. Psalm 137 laments the destruction of Jerusalem by praying that God will curse the psalmist if he ever forgets the events. The psalm then ends powerfully by asking God to bless those who crush the skulls of Babylonian babies against the rocks of the Tigris and Euphrates. One cannot find a more powerful and human expression of grief coupled with desire for revenge than this—at least in the TNK.

The Exile caused not only emotional trauma, but also theological. The ancient Jewish people, much as we do today in the aftermath of horrible events natural or otherwise, asked a series of religious questions: Wasn't God powerful enough to keep this from happening? Has God broken covenant with us? Why us—why are *we* suffering? The first question would have taken what seems an odd form to us, for it would have been asked something like this: "Is Marduk (the name of the chief god in the Babylonian pantheon) more powerful than YHWH (the name of the Jewish God)?" At the time at which the Exile occurred, the ancient world was henotheistic, which means that people believed every nation had its own god or set of gods. It was also widely believed that if one nation defeated another it meant that the victor's gods (in this case, Babylon's) were more powerful than the gods of the vanquished (in this case, Israel's God).

A second question presupposes Jewish identity, which revolves around three covenants: those made between God and Abraham, God and the Israelites at Sinai, and God and David. In Genesis 12, God issues the first iteration of a promise to Abraham in which God promises to give Abraham a homeland and a large number of descendants, who will then become a means of blessing the world. This promise suggests, at the very least, that the ancient Hebrews were a people chosen for a mission. In the next covenant, mediated by Moses at Sinai, the Israelites who had escaped from Egypt enter into a relationship with God in which they pledge to make this God (the one who rescued them) their God in return for God's blessings and ongoing protection. In doing so, they promise to obey a series of laws that stipulate the requirements of the relationship. The final covenant is one God makes with David in II Samuel 7 and is sometimes called the Davidic or Royal Covenant because God promises that a descendant of David will rule on the throne of Jerusalem forever. The Exile would have raised the question of what has happened to this relationship. Has God broken covenant? What are we to make of the fact that there is no throne left in Jerusalem, and David's last descendant is in Babylon?

A third question raised by the exiles follows from the second: "If God has broken covenant, why?" Put differently, "What did we do to deserve exile?" As we will see, at least four answers emerge over the development of the TNK. The first is "We deserved it," a view associated with what is often called the Deuteronomistic history (the books of Joshua, Judges, I Samuel, II Samuel, I Kings and II Kings). This literature answers the question by saying that the Exile is punishment for disobedience. The second, associated with the second part of Isaiah, is that while bad things can happen to innocent people, those events can lead to greater good. This view is developed using the literary device of the Suffering Servant, God's servant who is obedient and faithful, yet rejected and beaten.[4] The result, however, is said to be the healing of others. The third and fourth are both given voice in the book of Job.[5] The prologue of the book suggests that suffering is a test to see if one's faith is genuine. Later, God admits to creating a world that is chaotic, a statement that suggests that humans are not the center of the universe and that God does not exist to guarantee human well-being.

The Exile continues until the Persian Empire displaces the Babylonians in 538 BCE and Cyrus of Persia issues an edict that allows the Jewish people to return to Judah, which is now a vassal state of Persia. The relatively benign rule of the Persians is followed by the rise of the Greek empire under Alexander the Great, which goes reasonably well until his successor, Antiochus IV, bedevils the Jewish people and motivates the Maccabean revolt in 167 BCE, leading to a brief time of relative independence for the Jewish people until the Roman conquest in 63 BCE.

In short, the Exile and its aftermath are hardly idyllic. Perhaps Donn Morgan describes this post-Exilic world best when he says:

> Within many communities (e.g., Babylon, Egypt, Jerusalem) where Jews now resided there was a religious pluralism so extreme it threatened the very continuity of Israel. There was no single definition of Israel, no single notion of how Israel should be constituted, or should relate to foreign powers, or should govern itself. The identity of Israel was a central question.... Perhaps most importantly, there was no single definition of God.... There was no king, no monarchical state. There was no autonomy of the people, and this clearly was not going to change for the foreseeable future...Never again would all the worshippers of Yahweh live in the same land.[6]

William P. Brown echoes Morgan by characterizing the time as a precarious one in which there was no functioning government, violence and theft were rampant, debt was accumulating in significant amounts, people lived in crushing poverty, and the community was racked by ethnic conflict.[7]

The TNK thus to some extent represents ancient Israel's attempt to re-create itself in the "cultures wars" that erupt in the aftermath of the political/religious/existential devastation of Exile. In the way that these books are put together (regardless of their individual origins), the TNK narrates the story from optimistic beginnings to the realization that the world is not as simple as was once believed. The Promise to Abraham, to which the people of Israel trace their origins, has not been fulfilled, at least in any easy, straightforward way. God does not always seem to act as one thinks God ought to act. The world is a hostile place, as evidenced especially by the early experience with Egypt and reinforced now by successive domination by Assyria, Babylon, and Greece. Thus it seems that life can be hard and cruel, and what is left of Israel at the end of Exile is therefore left wondering how to go on and live as God's people in such a world. This becomes especially apparent in the Writings, which we will see contains a mix of diverse viewpoints that do not easily reconcile with each other, let alone with the views of Torah and Prophets. It is a world that requires wisdom to negotiate.

The first step, then, in this thought experiment is to give history its due in understanding these texts. It is a history that has many gaps, but one in which the Exile plays a significant role. When we talk about the collection of these texts, we begin to talk about canon, which takes us to the second step in this experiment.

Reading These Texts as Canon

The term canon comes from the Greek word meaning "reed," as in the tall plant that grows in shallow water. In the ancient world, reeds were sometimes used as measuring sticks. Metaphorically, to call a collection of literature "canon" is to say that it serves as a shared standard of measurement. In the case of Jewish and Christian traditions, the books of the canon, at their best, set the standard for discerning an authentic word about God and life under God. As we will see, however, the canon does not do so in a straightforward way, in part because it contains texts written by different authors facing different problems at different times in history. Still, these discrete documents can be, and have been, put together in different ways to tell different stories that serve as guides for different purposes.

Consider how the Christian Old Testament tells a different story than the TNK. When Christianity emerged in the first century CE, it began as a movement within Judaism. As this movement produced its own literature, such as epistles and gospels that later would comprise what is called the New Testament, the early Christians continued to read and reflect on the sacred texts of Judaism.[8] In doing so, the early Christians took the Jewish scriptures and rearranged them, renaming them as Old Testament (see the chart below). In looking at the chart on the next page, note first that Christians took the three-part structure of the Hebrew Scriptures and turned it into four: the Pentateuch (a Greek word for five scrolls), History, Poetry/Wisdom, and Prophecy. In doing so, they also recategorized some books. Most notably, Daniel moved from Writings to Prophecy, and the books of Ruth and Esther moved from Writings to History. Even more important than this reclassification of documents is how the early church changed the story that they tell.

This change is especially apparent in how the two collections end. The Old Testament concludes with the prophetic book of Malachi, which looks forward to the time when someone will announce the coming Day of the Lord. The New Testament begins by interpreting John the Baptist as that figure who then announces the coming of Jesus as the Lord. Thus the Christian Old Testament begins a story that is fulfilled in the New Testament. In contrast, the TNK concludes with II Chronicles, which ends with Cyrus of Persia's edict of restoration. This edict marks the end of the Babylonian Exile and allows the Jewish people to return to their homeland and rebuild their lives. Thus the TNK ends by looking to a future for God's people as a re-established nation state. TNK and Old Testament, by the way they order the documents that make them up, thus tell different stories—and these may not be the only stories they tell, as that depends on the question we bring to the canon as we read it.

Reading these texts in the order they appear in the TNK better allows us to see how they tell a story of moral development that culminates with wisdom. The Law begins with stories in which God and people do not always act in ways that see good. It concludes with the covenant at Sinai, a covenant characterized by the giving of hundreds of laws intended to govern behavior of both God and the Israelites. The Prophets carry on the story of the ancient Jewish people after the giving of the laws, and in so doing describe how the ancient Israelites do not do very well at keeping the laws (something that is true of all of us, even today).

The Contents of the TNK and Old Testament Compared

TNK (Hebrew Scriptures)

Torah/Law

Genesis
Exodus
Leviticus
Numbers
Deuteronomy

Nevi'im/Prophets

Former Prophets:

Joshua
Judges
Samuel
Kings

Latter Prophets:

Isaiah
Jeremiah
Ezekiel
The Twelve:

Hosea	Nahum
Amos	Habakkuk
Micah	Zephaniah
Joel	Haggai
Obadiah	Zechariah
Jonah	Malachi

Kethuvim/Writings

Psalms
Proverbs
Job
Song of Songs
Ruth
Lamentations
Ecclesiastes
Esther
Daniel
Ezra-Nehemiah
Chronicles

The Old Testament (not including Apocrypha)

Pentateuch

Genesis
Exodus
Leviticus
Numbers
Deuteronomy

History

Joshua
Judges
Ruth
I and II Samuel
I and II Kings
I and II Chronicles
Ezra
Nehemiah
Esther

Poetry and Wisdom

Job
Psalms
Proverbs
Ecclesiastes
Song of Songs

Prophets

Isaiah	Micah
Jeremiah	Nahum
Lamentations	Habakkuk
Ezekiel	Zephaniah
Daniel	Haggai
Hosea	Zechariah
Joel	Malachi
Amos	
Obadiah	
Jonah	

Later prophets begin to appeal to internalized principles as the basis for moral behavior, but this seems to be no more effective than appealing to explicit laws. The Writings, as we will see in Chapter 4, present readers with a set of conflicting perspectives on a variety of topics framed by wisdom's invitation in Proverbs. In reading the Old Testament as TNK, readers are encouraged to consider the relative value of rules (or laws) and principles as the basis for morality and are enjoined, instead of relying solely on either, to develop wisdom.

Judaism and the Law

In saying that the Law represents an attempt to build a morality around rules or laws, we must be careful to be clear on this point. Given the long history of Christian stereotypes that Judaism is a religion of law and Christianity is a religion of grace, it would be easy to think that I am reinforcing this stereotype. *Nothing could be further from the truth, as careful readers will see.* According to the way of reading the Hebrew Bible I suggest in this work, moral development may begin with "law," but the developing tradition, in narrative sections of Law, as well as Prophets and Writings, calls into question an exclusive, legalistic focus on law. Thus the canonical texts themselves offer their own internal critique of legalism. Moreover, later developments in the period between the testaments equate wisdom with the law. Thus, on this reading of the TNK, the Jewish tradition, at its best, comes full circle to appreciate the law with what we might call a post-critical naiveté.

Unfortunately, both Christian and Western history have too often devalued law in our attempts to get away from authoritarianism. Gospel writers too often portray ancient Judaism as legalistic by setting up conflicts between Pharisees and Jesus over keeping the law, in which Jesus too readily emerges as "the hero." Martin Luther's interpretation of Paul's letters has steered generations of Christians into believing that Paul rejected Jewish law. At least since Kant's call—"Dare to think for yourselves!"—westerners have rejected external authority in a quest for autonomy. Of course, in perpetuating these stereotypes, we conveniently ignore how Jesus himself honors— even intensifies—the law, how Jesus' teaching is comparable to that of some other rabbis of his day, how Paul champions the law, and how external authority is unavoidable in life. As Richard Rohr puts it, "Without law in some form, and also without butting up against that law, we cannot move forward easily and naturally."[1]

continued on page 12

continued from page 11

For Further Reading

For brief treatments of the religious side of these issues, see the following articles in the *Jewish Annotated New Testament* (New York: Oxford University Press, 2011):
—Shaye J.D. Cohen, "Judaism and Jewishness," pp. 513-515.
—Susannah Heschel, "Jesus in Modern Jewish Thought," pp. 582-585.
—Jonathan Klawans, "The Law," pp. 515-519.
—Daniel R. Langston, "Paul in Jewish Thought," pp. 585-587.
—Mark D. Nanos, "Paul and Judaism," pp. 551.

On western society's rejection of authority, see Jeffrey Stout, *The Flight from Authority* (Notre Dame: University of Notre Dame Press, 1981).

[1]Richard Rohr, *Falling Upward: A Spirituality for the Two Halves of Life* (San Francisco: Jossey-Bass, 2011), 25.

Reading These Texts Naively

The final step in reading the Old Testament for the purposes of this book, then, is to read these texts naively. Doing so encourages us to focus only on what we as readers know from the text itself rather than bringing our preexisting knowledge and attitudes to the text. When we do so, we risk reading into the text things that might not be there. Take Abraham, for example. In an episode that we will look at later, he lies about the identity of his wife by telling Pharaoh that Sarah is his sister. Historical investigation could help us discover the customs in the ancient world that might make this action intelligible. As readers of the text, however, we are not told what those customs are; we are left uninformed. Rather than try to infer what those customs might be, for purposes of this book we will simply take the stories at face value.

To read the texts naively does not, however, mean reading them without thinking. While we will take the stories at face value, we can still attend to matters of characterization, plot development, and literary devices. For example, in treating figures such as Abraham, we will concentrate on what we can infer about his character based on how the author(s)/editor(s) of the text narrate his actions. Sometimes Abraham exhibits significant faith and trust in God, and at other times he does not. Sometimes he learns from his mistakes, and at other times he does not. The composite picture of Abraham is therefore that he is neither unambiguously saint nor sinner. Instead, he is, like all of us, a bit of both.

Put somewhat differently, I ask that we read the biblical texts with a "post-critical naiveté" that attends primarily to the profound truths embodied in these stories while largely, but not entirely, bracketing questions of historical truth.[9] What this means is that I will be asking us to consider how texts might be true even if the events depicted in them may not be historically accurate. I realize that this is an odd way of reading the texts and again do not mean to imply that this is the only way to read the TNK—a literary analysis can certainly be informed fruitfully by historical and other forms of analysis. However, I ask the reader to recall that we are engaged in a thought experiment in which the payoff will be the value of the insights we gain into the TNK and moral development.

Looking Back and Looking Ahead

In this chapter, I have invited readers to begin the process of developing wisdom by reading the Old Testament in a particular way. Put differently, I have issued an invitation to engage in a thought experiment that requires us to read the Old Testament from a different, definitely strange, and probably (at least initially) uncomfortable perspective. Drawing from the history behind the texts, I invite us to read as people in the contested post-Exilic era might have done. Put differently, we will seek to indwell their situation imaginatively and try to empathize with them. In doing so, we may well find that imagination and empathy turn out to be key elements in wisdom. Drawing from the status of these texts as canon, I invite us to read them as telling a story about moral development. Finally, I invite us to read the texts naively while still attending to the artistry found in them.

Earlier, I said that canon typically means a standard for determining what is an authentic word about God. The TNK does not provide a simple standard, for what it does is require us to engage questions that have no easy answers. Moreover, it requires readers to participate in struggles over what to do with dissenting views. The canon does not silence dissenters; instead, it preserves their voices and keeps them as participants in the community. In this way, we are reminded that this collection, whether

TNK or Old Testament, is Jewish literature, produced by the people of Israel, a word which means something like, "One who wrestles with God and lives to tell about it the next day."[10] Or as Elie Wiesel once put it, "You can be a Jew with God and you can be a Jew against God. You can't be a Jew without God."[11] The TNK thus represents an argument of sorts, one that invites us to develop wisdom by actively participating in it.[12]

Enough preliminaries. In the next chapter, we will explore the moral story found in the Law.

Questions for Discussion

1. This chapter opens by claiming that we need wisdom, not just information. Do you agree or disagree? Explain.

2. In reading novels or watching movies, we have to "willingly suspend disbelief" to enter into the world created by the text. The thought experiment of this book asks us to do the same with texts regarded by many as sacred or holy scripture. What excites you about doing so? What worries you about doing so?

3. I suggest in note 3 that recalling the events of 9/11 and our responses to it might help us understand how devastating the Exile was to the ancient Jewish people. Reflect again on those attacks. How have they changed our world and our perceptions of it?

4. The quotation from Donn Morgan highlights the pluralism of the post-Exilic world. Does that description sound anything like our current situation? Explain.

Endnotes

[1]We will examine both ancient and contemporary accounts of wisdom in greater detail in Chapter 5.

[2]I follow the long-standing academic convention of using CE (Common Era) and BCE (Before the Common Era) for dates rather than the popular BC (Before Christ) and AD (*anno domini*, that is, in the year of our Lord).

[3]It may be helpful to get a sense of the significance of the Exile by recalling how the terrorists of September 11, 2001 struck symbols of U.S. economic power (the World Trade Center) and military power (the Pentagon), and were presumably headed for the seat of political power (the White House or Congress).

[4]This description is a composite drawn from Isaiah 42:1-4, 49:1-6, 50:4-11, and 52:13-53:12.

[5]Whether or not Job is written to answer this question is a matter of debate among biblical scholars. We will treat Job at greater length in Chapter Four.

[6]Donn F. Morgan, *The Making of Sages: Biblical Wisdom and Contemporary Culture* (Harrisburg, PA: Trinity Press), 120-121.

[7]William P. Brown, *Wisdom's Wonder: Character, Creation, and Crisis in the Bible's Wisdom Literature* (Grand Rapids, MI: William B. Eerdmans Publishing Co., 2014), 40-41.

[8]This is not to say that all Christians agreed on the value of these texts, for the early Christians also argued over the relative value of the Old Testament for Christian faith. One sees this in the Pauline epistles in the New Testament, especially in Galatians and Romans, where Paul and his opponents argue over how much of the Jewish scriptures one must follow to be a Christian. Debates continued in the 2nd century CE when Marcion published a list of Christian scriptures that left out the Old Testament entirely. In response, the Church reaffirmed the place of the Old Testament in Christian faith.

[9]On post-critical naiveté, see Marcus Borg, *Reading the Bible Again for the First Time* (New York: HarperCollins, 2001), 49-51.

[10]In Genesis 32:23-33, Jacob's name is changed to Israel after he wrestles with a stranger.

[11]Elie Wiesel, in "Judaism: The Chosen People." *The Long Search.* By Ronald Eyre. Ambrose Video: 1977.

[12]Eugene Garver discusses how participating in an argument can create a community in his *For the Sake of Argument: Practical Reasoning, Character, and the Ethics of Belief* (Chicago: University of Chicago Press, 2004). See especially 33-34 and 80. Much as he says that the Constitution of the United States is where we find a statement of the American *ethos*, I submit that the TNK serves as a window into the Jewish and Christian *ethos*.

CHAPTER TWO

Rules as Response to Need for Order

An Overview of the Law

The term "Torah" is often translated from the Hebrew as "Law," which is a fair enough description at one level of analysis because much of the material in the books that comprise the Law (Genesis, Exodus, Leviticus, Numbers, and Deuteronomy) is legal in nature. Much of Exodus and Deuteronomy, as well as all of Leviticus, consists of laws that spell out—in sometimes tedious detail—how the ancient Israelites should order their lives in relation to one another, the world, and God. However, a better translation of Torah is "instruction," as this literature also consists of many narrative sections that recite a number of stories. Although these stories were written at different times by different authors and existed independently of each other prior to their collection around the time of the Exile, their sequence follows a broad narrative arc within which we find a story of moral development, at least when read with our driving question in mind (see the sidebar on the next page for a guide to the literary history of what becomes the Torah). I begin with an overview of this narrative arc before giving focal attention to some selections that highlight moral development.

Broadly speaking, Genesis 1-11 tells ancient Israel's stories of the origins of the world and is sometimes referred to as the primeval history. Genesis 12-50 tells stories of Israel's ancestors, especially Abraham and Sarah, Isaac and Rebekah, Jacob (whose name is later changed to Israel) and his wives (Leah and Rachel) and concubines (Zilpah and Bilhah), and Joseph. These stories tell the fate of God's promise to give Abraham

A Quick Guide to the Documentary Hypothesis

The history of the sources that make up the Torah has been the subject of Source Criticism. According to this reconstruction, the five books of the Torah have been edited together from four different sources:

—The earliest is the Yahwistic source (abbreviated J), which dates to around 950 BCE, the era of Solomon's reign.

—The next is the Elohistic source (abbreviated E), which dates to around 750 BCE, the time of the divided monarchy.

—Then comes the Deuteronomic source (abbreviated D), which dates to around 620 BCE, after the Assyrian capture of Israel that left Judah as the remaining portion of the once independent Israel.

—The final source is called the Priestly source (abbreviated P), which dates to around 550 BC, the time of the Exile.

Most often associated with the works of Karl H. Graf and Julius Wellhausen in the 19th century, this view has been debated endlessly. Still, most scholars use some version of the Documentary Hypothesis to explain the pre-canonical roots of these books.

land and descendants and to make his people a blessing to the world. As Genesis ends, Abraham has a few descendants and Joseph ends up being a blessing to his family and the Egyptians, but Abraham's descendants are living in Egypt, not the Promised Land.

Exodus picks up the story several generations after Joseph's death and depicts a time when Pharaoh enslaves the Israelites because they are perceived as threats to Egypt. Moses eventually confronts Pharaoh and, after a lengthy series of events, leads the Israelites out of Egypt and into the wilderness. Eventually they make their way to Mount Sinai, where the Israelites enter into a formal relationship with the God who delivers them from Egypt. The story of the covenant, first found in Exodus 20-34 (and later expanded in Deuteronomy 5-28), depicts the Israelites as making a suzerainty covenant in which they pledge allegiance to YHWH by agreeing to obey the laws that YHWH gives them. In return, God promises to bless them if they keep the laws and punish them if they break them. The laws then make up the bulk of the material found in the rest of Exodus and the entire book of Leviticus. The book of Numbers tells the story of the people setting out from Sinai into the wilderness toward the Promised Land—a journey that takes forty years, until the generation that experienced the Exodus dies.[1]

The book of Deuteronomy begins with the next generation of Israelites encamped east of the Jordan River, ready to enter the Promised Land of Canaan. The book, at face value, consists of three speeches by Moses in which he reminds the Israelites of all that God has done and of their own failings, then calls them to keep the covenant so that they will thrive in their new home. Unlike the story of the covenant in Exodus, Moses' retelling makes explicit that the Israelites will be blessed for adhering to the laws and punished for failing to keep them. In a sense, Deuteronomy represents a second try at the experiment of building morality around laws or rules. Here, God tries with a different population—the descendants of those who experienced the Exodus—and also makes explicit the consequences of obedience and disobedience.[2]

This is the bare shape of the Law's narrative arc. Reading it with our driving question in mind (that is, "What is the story of moral development told by the TNK?") allows us to see nuances to this broad storyline that we might not otherwise notice. Looking at the Law with this question in mind, and playing off of the notion of "law," we discover that the Law falls into two primary sections. After a preface of sorts in Genesis 1:1-2:4a, the first major part of the Law describes life before the giving of the Law, and the second discusses the giving of the Law.

Here we consider some snapshots from Genesis and Exodus that point to the need for laws, or rules, to guide the behavior of both the human characters and even God. Readers should note that these snapshots do not exhaust the material that we could examine, but are instead meant to illustrate themes in the text that emerge when the text is read *literarily* as a continuous narrative (rather than *literally* as factually accurate in all details). Perhaps most troubling to readers will be how God comes across in the stories. In response, I remind readers that we need to distinguish between how the authors characterize God as a part of the story and claims about what God is really like.

Life Before Law

While the Law opens with two different creation stories (to which I will return later in this chapter and in Chapter 5), I want to begin with the story of Cain and Abel in Genesis 4:1-16 because it is a particularly clear example of the problem found in life before the giving of the laws at Sinai. After being banished from the Garden of Eden, Adam and Eve give birth to Cain and Abel, who grow up to take on different occupations, agriculture and animal husbandry, respectively. Both brothers bring an offering to God, who accepts Abel's gift but rejects Cain's. Cain becomes angry and kills Abel, thereby earning a curse from God, which is subsequently softened after Cain argues that the punishment is too great to bear.

What is left unsaid in this story is why any of the actors did what they did. As readers, we are not told why Cain offered some of his crops and Abel the "firstlings" of his animals (Genesis 4:4).[3] More troubling is that God does not seem to know what God wants and thus appears to act impulsively—with the consequence that Abel is dead and Cain is banished "from the presence of the Lord" (Genesis 4:16). Commentators traditionally offer the explanation that God rejected Cain's sacrifice because he did not bring the "first fruit" of the ground. Certainly the text bears such a reading since, aside from the different contents of the offering (produce vs. meat), it deliberately describes Abel's offerings as the firstlings. However, this explanation requires that readers import their preexisting ideas about God into the text. On narrative grounds, there is no reason to know that God prefers the firstlings. Based only on the information we have in these early chapters of Genesis, the actions of all parties remain curious, in part because there are no rules or instructions for them to follow.

Some might argue that I am leaving out the events of the previous chapter in which Adam and Eve eat the fruit from the tree of knowledge of good and evil. As such, then one should expect that both they and their offspring would know the right thing to do. In that episode, the serpent says that they will "be like the divine beings, knowing good and bad" (3:5). However, perhaps part of the serpent's lie is that it misrepresents

God, for at this point in the narrative, it is not clear that God even knows the difference between good and evil.[4] After all, in response to their failure, God moves almost immediately from cursing them (plus the serpent and the ground) to actions that indicate that God has overreacted: God clothes them, then exiles them from the Garden before they can eat of the tree of life. The result is that God seems to struggle with knowing how to respond to Adam and Eve's transgression.

Another place in which God does not seem to know what God wants to do is the flood story, which begins with the narrator informing us that God regrets creating human beings because they are always doing evil. In response, God decides to "blot out" not just humanity, but also *all* land animals and birds (Genesis 6:6-7). However, upon discovering that Noah "walked with God" (Genesis 6:9), God decides to preserve him and his family, along with some animals. The flood ensues, but notice what happens after the flood. Noah sacrifices an animal to God, who upon "smelling the pleasing odor" (Genesis 8:21) decides never again to destroy the earth. It is as if God realizes that the flood might have been an overreach once God smells cooking flesh! As if to make sure that God remembers this pledge, God sets a rainbow in the sky as a reminder both to God and humanity (Genesis 9:8-17). God, as a character in the story, again seems to be making things up as God goes along. There seems to be no plan, no sense of how to proceed. God is most often reactive rather than proactive. Like human beings, God seems to need guidelines for how to live, although with the rainbow—this external reminder to keep a promise—it does seem that God takes the first step in developing some self-discipline, some way of constraining apparently impulsive behavior.

Moving from the primeval stories to the ancestral stories, we see that the lack of concrete guides for action gets the ancestors in trouble, too. We meet the first of the ancestors, Abraham, in a genealogy in Genesis 11. There we learn that he is descended from Noah's son, Shem, and that his father is Terah. Abraham is married to Sarah, who suffers from infertility. They live in Ur, but at some point in time, Terah and his clan set out for Canaan. They settle, however, in Haran. In Genesis 12, Abraham responds to God's call to move on from Haran to Canaan. Abraham arrives quickly in the Promised Land, only to find famine there. He and

Sarah therefore head to Egypt to find sustenance. On the way, Abraham decides that it would be wise to introduce themselves as brother and sister rather than husband and wife so that the Egyptians will not kill him and take her for themselves. Pharaoh does indeed take Sarah into his harem and pays Abraham rather handsomely for doing so (Genesis 12:16). God then sends plagues on Pharaoh, who confronts Abraham and essentially asks him, "Why didn't you just tell me the truth? Don't you see how much trouble you've caused by lying to me?"

Although Pharaoh lets them go, Abraham does not seem to have learned from this narrow escape, for this plotline is repeated in Genesis 20.[5] This time, Abraham and Sarah go to Gerar to escape famine. Abraham again tells the king that Sarah is his sister, this time justifying the subterfuge by saying that it wasn't a complete lie because Sarah is his half-sister (20:12). Nevertheless, a half truth is not the whole truth, and the results, again, are less than happy. As readers, we can perhaps sympathize with Abraham's concerns for his safety, but we wonder about the wisdom of his actions. Does Abraham not know that lying is, at best, a dicey course of action? Of course, to be fair to Abraham, as readers of the text, we know of no prior instruction that prohibits lying.[6] Regardless, without rules, Abraham, as a character in the story, behaves in ways that lead to trouble, a pattern that continues in the stories of his descendants, Isaac, Jacob, and Joseph. The same is true of Moses, who is later "eulogized" as a prophet unlike any who came later (Deuteronomy 34:10-12).[7] Consider now some episodes from their stories.

Isaac's name literally means "son of laughter," because Sarah laughs at God's promise to let her have a son in her old age (Genesis 18:1-15). Despite being the child promised by God, Isaac never develops much as a character in the story. His part begins in Genesis 25:19, where we learn he marries Rebekah, who, like his mother, suffers from infertility. He prays that God will let them have children, which God does: twins, Esau and Jacob. Esau is the oldest—barely—and apparently a "manly man" who likes to hunt and be outdoors, whereas Jacob is a "girly man" who likes to stay close to home. Isaac and Rebekah play favorites, however, for Isaac favors Esau and Rebekah Jacob. Note especially the reason why Isaac favors Esau—he likes the taste of meat (Genesis 25:28)![8]

This favoritism creates problems later in the story, when Rebekah persuades Jacob to disguise himself as Esau to trick an old and blind Isaac out of the blessing typically due to the firstborn. Earlier in the story, in a private communication to Rebekah, God tells her that Esau will serve Jacob (see Genesis 25:22-23).[9] Rebekah does not seem to have shared this information with Isaac, however, which means that Isaac is unknowingly ignoring God's wishes. It also means that Rebekah manipulates the succession of Jacob over Esau, rather than letting God's plan work out on its own. The result of this subterfuge is that Esau vows to kill Jacob, and so Rebekah advises Jacob to leave the Promised Land—all of which calls into question the fate of the initial promise to Abraham (Genesis 27:41-45).[10]

While there is much more that can be said about Jacob, I focus on this issue of favoritism and the seeming inability of the ancestors to learn from their experiences. Just as Jacob's parents played favorites, so too does Jacob. He favors Joseph, the first son of the second wife—a fact that is readily apparent to Joseph's brothers and strains their relationships. As the text puts it, "they hated him so that they could not speak a friendly word to him" (Genesis 37:4). Of course, Joseph hardly helps his case because he not only has a dream in which his brothers all bow down to him, he rubs their noses in it! The result is that the brothers conspire to kill Joseph but instead sell him into slavery. He ends up in Egypt where, after several turns of events, he becomes a trusted advisor to Pharaoh and manages to help Egypt—and the entire region—weather a severe famine. When word gets out that Egypt has food, Joseph's family travels there to seek assistance. Joseph toys with them, demanding at one point that his full brother, Benjamin (by Rachel and Jacob), be held as ransom. Eventually, Joseph reveals his identity to the brothers and the whole clan migrates to Egypt, where they survive the crisis. Everything seems to work out fine in the end, but the process has been far from smooth. Joseph ends up being a blessing to both his family and the Egyptians, but it does sometimes seem to be in spite of himself.

The next major figure we meet in the Law is Moses, who leads the Israelites out of slavery in Egypt and acts as the mediator who communicates God's law to the people. But we see that he is himself sometimes out of control. An Israelite who grows up in Pharaoh's household, he sees an Egyptian beating a Hebrew slave and impulsively kills the Egyptian. Does Moses not know that murder is wrong? How can he, however, since the commandment prohibiting murder has not yet been revealed?

Moses then flees for his life to Midian, where he is eventually confronted by the odd sight of a burning bush. There he experiences God's call to confront Pharaoh and lead the Israelites out of Egypt to Canaan. But instead of responding obediently, Moses starts making excuses—five of them, each of which God rebuts (Exodus 3:11-4:17). The first excuse is, "I'm a nobody—a fugitive murderer. Who am *I* to confront Pharaoh?" God replies that Moses is the one God has chosen for this task. In the second, Moses says, "I need to be able to tell folks who sent me, so that folks will know that I am not doing this on my own." God tells Moses to say that it is the God of the ancestors who sent him. In the third, Moses asks, "But what if they don't believe me?" God turns Moses' rod into a snake and tells Moses that he can offer similar signs to convince skeptics. In the fourth, Moses claims that he is not a good public speaker, to which God replies that God can empower him. Finally, Moses begs God to find someone else to do the job. God, getting a bit angry at this point, decides to let Aaron do the talking, so long as Moses writes the speeches.[11]

Moses later does what God asks, but still there are some rough edges. In the journey from Egypt to Mount Sinai, Moses finally tires of dealing with the whining Israelites and, apparently fearful of a riot in which he will be killed, demands answers from God, saying, in effect, "What am I supposed to do now with this obstinate bunch of people?" (Exodus 17:4). A bit later, when God is ready to annihilate the Israelites, Moses steps in to pray on their behalf, reminding God that God's reputation among the Egyptians would be mud if God were to wipe out the Israelites now. Moses also reminds God of all the promises made to Abraham and the other ancestors (Exodus 32:9-14). In sum, Moses, like the ancestors, comes across as a fully human character—sometimes noble, sometimes brash, sometimes cowardly—whose life might have gone more smoothly if there had been explicit rules or guidelines to follow.

To recap: the first part of the Law describes how people act impulsively, as if they don't know what to do, thereby creating problems for themselves and others. Cain kills Abel. Abraham lies about his wife—twice. Isaac and Rebekah play favorites. Moses commits murder. This impulsiveness is true even of God, who overreacts to Adam and Eve's misdeeds in the Garden of Eden and the "evil" that leads God to flood the earth—only later to repent of both acts. God would have destroyed the Israelites in the wilderness had Moses not intervened. Everyone, it seems, could benefit from having clearer expectations about how to live with one another. And so, in Exodus 20, we finally get those expectations.

The Law Itself

As noted earlier, the narrative context of the giving of the Law follows the pattern of ancient suzereignty covenants in which a king accepts as his people those who pledge to keep the stipulations that define that relationship. In this case, God is the king who accepts the Israelites as his people. In accepting God's acceptance of them, the Israelites promise to keep the provisions of the covenant (the laws).[12] In return, God promises to protect and provide for them. Regardless of when the laws were actually written, in the narrative context the laws are all given by God, thus signaling to readers their gravitas. Given what we have seen previously in the narrative, the laws also promise to guide not only the actions of the Israelites, but also of God, thus bringing some order out of the chaos of not knowing clearly what is good or bad, right or wrong.

One thing that strikes the reader is how comprehensive the laws are. Scholars traditionally divide the contents of the law into three categories.[13] First comes the moral law, the Ten Commandments (literally "Words"), that in some ways are broad enough to be universal, in that every culture finds a way to regulate these behaviors that govern relationship to the divine and to the neighbor, the so-called two tables of the Law (see the chart on the next page).

Second come judicial laws that govern relations in society, such as how to treat different groups of slaves (Exodus 21:2-11) and what to do when my ox gores your ox (Exodus 21:28-32). The third group of laws are often labeled ceremonial laws because they instruct people on how to worship God properly (e.g., Exodus 24:12-31:18 and Leviticus 1-7). The basic function appears to be that the laws, at their best, represent an

The Two Tables of the Law

Some commentators prefer to say that "the Ten Commandments" are not laws, as such, but broader principles that the rest of the laws then explain/ unpack. Regardless, commentators agree that there are two tables to the law. The first table typically is understood to identify one's obligations to God and the second one's obligations to the neighbor. Scholars disagree on how to divide the Ten Commandments among the two tables.

Roman Catholic/Lutheran

First Table: Duties to God

- You shall have no other gods (Exodus 20:1-6)
- You shall not swear falsely (Exodus 20:7)
- You shall keep the Sabbath holy (Exodus 20:8-11)

Second Table: Duties to Neighbor

- Honor father and mother (Exodus 20:12)
- You shall not murder (Exodus 20:13)
- You shall not commit adultery (Exodus 20:13)
- You shall not steal (Exodus 20:13)
- You shall not bear false witness (Exodus 20:13)
- You shall not covet your neighbor's house (Exodus 20:14a)
- You shall not covet your neighbor's wife, etc. (Exodus 20:14b)

Reformed

First Table: Duties to God

- You shall have no other gods (Exodus 20:1-3)
- You shall not make a sculpted image (Exodus 20:4-6)
- You shall not swear falsely (Exodus 20:7)
- You shall keep the Sabbath holy (Exodus 20:8-11)

Second Table: Duties to Neighbor

- Honor father and mother (Exodus 20:12)
- You shall not murder (Exodus 20:13)
- You shall not commit adultery (Exodus 20:13)
- You shall not steal (Exodus 20:13)
- You shall not bear false witness (Exodus 20:13)
- You shall not covet your neighbor's house, wife, etc. (Exodus 20:14)

attempt to bring all of life into relationship with God, thereby making explicit the expectations and responsibilities for which both God and the Israelites can be held accountable.

Hints of That Which Is to Come

As I have told this story about the Law, one would expect life after Law to work out fine. After all, both God and people now know what has to be done to live in relation to one another. Astute readers will note, however, that even the Law itself plants doubts about how this experiment will turn out. I will mention two. Consider the story of Adam, Eve, and the Serpent in Genesis 2:4b-3:24.[14] In this version of the creation story, God creates a single person from the dust of the earth and places him in the Garden. He is told to till and keep the garden and to eat the fruit from any tree except the tree of the knowledge of good and evil. If he does eat of that tree, he will die (Genesis 2:4b-9, 15-16). In short, we have two rules governing the care of the environment and diet. The rules do not, however, prevent a descent into chaos, for their meaning is open to misunderstanding and requires interpretation.

This is what happens when the Serpent tempts Eve, who has already added a prohibition to the original commandment. She thinks that they are forbidden even to touch the tree of the knowledge of good and evil (Genesis 3:3). The Serpent then asks, for all practical purposes, "What does it mean to die?" Eve thinks one thing, presumably physical death, whereas the Serpent suggests that what dying means is not physical death but that they will become like God (Genesis 3:5). At that point, Eve eats the forbidden fruit and gives some to Adam, with the result that they and the serpent are cursed, and then Adam and Eve are cast out of the garden (Genesis 3:14-24). In this situation, knowledge of the rules did not guarantee that they would be obeyed.

Consider, too, the stories of the making of the Covenant and the Israelites' time in the wilderness as they move from Sinai to the Promised Land. As noted above, the Israelites gather at Mt. Sinai and enter into and ratify a covenant with God (Exodus 20:1-24:11). As the narrative continues, Moses ascends the mountain to receive further instructions and spends considerable time there, enough time that the people begin to think he is not coming back (Exodus 24:12-32:14). Despite their pledge not to worship other gods (the first of the Ten Commandments), they demand that Aaron, Moses' brother and co-leader, make them a god that they can see, a task Aaron seems to do without hesitation. Once the Israelites leave Sinai, knowing the law and having pledged again to uphold it, things do not go well. The people complain bitterly about how rough life is in the wilderness (Numbers 11 and 20). They are fearful of what they find when they scout out the Promised Land (Numbers 13-14). A man breaks the Sabbath (Numbers 15:32-36). There are at least two rebellions against Moses' leadership (Numbers 16). Moses himself seems to start to believe he is God, in Numbers 20:1-13. In that episode, the people, whining and thirsty again, attribute the Exodus to Moses and Aaron, not God. Not only does Moses not correct them, but he implies that it is in his and Aaron's power to provide the water when he asks the people, "Shall *we* give you water from the rock?" God does indeed provide the water but prohibits Moses and Aaron from leading the Israelites into the Promised Land.

In short, reading the Law with our driving question in mind, the primary movement of the story is from the chaos that occurs without rules to guide expectations and behavior to God's provision of such guidelines. But there is a subtext as well, for portions of the text foreshadow what is to come. We get glimpses that knowledge of the law does not guarantee obedience. Nor does knowledge of the law settle all questions of application or interpretation. If the Law can indeed be read legitimately as an experiment in building a morality around laws, then it also contains hints that the prospects for success do not look good. The next section of the TNK, the Prophets, bears out this concern.

Questions for Discussion

1. Read Genesis 2-11, paying special attention to God's decisions. Are they wise? Explain. What makes an action wise, in your estimation? Discuss this matter with someone else. After consideration of what others have said, does your estimation of what is wise change? If so, how and why? If not, why not?

2. Read Genesis 22:1-19, the story often called "the binding of Isaac." Here Abraham, at God's command, prepares to sacrifice Isaac, the first and long-awaited of the many descendants promised to Abraham by God. Consider that Abraham has disobeyed God's dictates as often as he has obeyed them (recall all the drama around Hagar and Ishmael in Genesis 16 and 21 after Sarah tries to get an heir one way or another, only to change her mind about it once Hagar gets pregnant). Note, too, that Abraham had earlier persuaded God not to destroy Sodom and Gomorrah if there were ten innocent people there (Genesis 18:20-32). Does Abraham similarly protest to save Isaac's life? Is this wise? Explain. What makes an action wise, in your estimation? After consideration of what others have said, does your estimation of what is wise change? If so, how and why? If not, why not?

3. We have noted that God, Isaac/Rebekah, and Joseph all play favorites. Is that wise? Explain. What makes an action wise, in your estimation? After consideration of what others have said, does your estimation of what is wise change? If so, how and why? If not, why not?

4. According to this reading of the Law, life is portrayed as chaotic when there are not clear guidelines for action. Have you experienced anything like that? Describe the situation.

5. According to this reading of the Law, knowing rules is not enough to guarantee that people will follow them. Describe some instances when you have seen this. Do you find yourself ignoring rules? When? Why? What were the results?

6. I suggested above that one challenge of rules is knowing how to interpret or apply them. Take, for example, the laws in the Law that govern
   taking human life. One law prohibits murder (Exodus 20:13), while
   others allow for capital punishment in a number of circumstances
   (see, for example, Exodus 21:12-16 and 28-29). How do these texts
   distinguish between times in which taking a human life is allowed
   and when it is not? How do you evaluate those distinctions?

7. After reading this chapter, what do you see as the pros and cons of
   treating morality as a matter of following rules?

Endnotes

[1]The number forty is probably best understood to mean a complete period of time, rather than an actual number of years. Thus, we should understand that the Israelites wandered in the wilderness as long as it took for that generation to die.

[2]In Kohlberg's terms, such a strategy could represent the first level of moral reasoning in which good and bad, right and wrong are defined in light of the consequences to the self: If I benefit, it is good. It might also reflect the second level, in that good and bad, right and wrong are defined by external authorities.

[3]All quotations from the Hebrew Bible in this book come from the Tanakh translation of the Jewish Publication Society, in the *Jewish Study Bible* (New York: Oxford University Press), 2004.

[4]See Jack Miles, *God: A Biography* (New York: Vintage Books, 1995), 35-36. For more on this story in Genesis 3, see later in this chapter where I treat it as foreshadowing of what comes next.

[5]Scholars typically explain this repetition by arguing that the two stories come from different sources, but in canonical form, the repetition of the plot line leads us to wonder about Abraham's ability to learn from experience.

[6]In saying this, I do not assume that this reading exhausts the story. We could speculate about Abraham's motives and whether rules other than lying apply. As to motives, for example, Abraham may want to get rid of Sarah and stay in Egypt, or go on without her. He might be doing this as a way to get money—in effect, pimping his wife. Regardless of the possibilities, however, it is clear that his motives are not noble. As to "rules" that could conceivably apply to this situation, Abraham might think that there is a rule to preserve one's own self, or a "rule" that defines when a lie is justified or not, or rules that prioritize one rule over another in case of conflict. My point is simply that, taking the text at face value, Abraham clearly lies, and there are no prior instructions about truth-telling in the text. The commandment "you shall not bear false witness"—if it even refers to a condemnation of all lying—does not come until Exodus.

[7]Their foibles certainly do not prevent the ancestors from becoming iconic figures in Jewish and Christian thought, but the authors of these stories certainly do not hide the darker sides of these characters. The result is that the ancestors come across as complex and interesting people—much like real human beings, who are, to borrow Martin Luther's language, *simil justus et peccator*, both saint and sinner at the same time.

[8]There is a striking parallelism between these ancestors' actions and God's. Just as God plays favorites in choosing Abraham from among all the peoples of the earth, Isaac and Rebekah play favorites. Moreover, the reason for Isaac's preference for Esau recalls God's preference for Abel's offering over Cain's. Both are apparently carnivores! Isaac imitates not only God, but also his father by trying to pass off Rebekah as his sister (Genesis 26:1-11). Apparently the son does not learn from the mistakes of the father.

[9]One of the interesting thematic patterns in the TNK is a preference for the younger son over the older.

[10]The brothers do reconcile, however, much later in the narrative, when Esau graciously welcomes Jacob back into Canaan after several years in the "far country" (see Genesis 32).

[11]Some biblical traditions also list their sister Miriam as a co-leader of the Exodus. See, for example, Micah 6:4. She is also called a prophet in Exodus 15:20.

[12]The laws are contained in three primary collections, the first of which is called the Covenant Code because it is associated with the story of the covenant in Exodus 20:1-23:19. The second is the Holiness Code in Leviticus 17-26, which describes how the people are to be holy, i.e., distinct from other peoples, because their God is not like the gods of those other nations. The third code is the Deuteronomic Code of Deuteronomy 12-26. Scholars agree that the laws were not written at this point in Israelite history, but do not agree on when the laws were actually written.

[13]To be sure, there is a bit of slippage in these traditional terms, but they do provide a useful, if limited, classification scheme.

[14]This story is often called the Yahwistic creation story, in part because it refers to God as Yahweh and is usually considered part of the J source. It is dramatically different in detail from the story of Genesis 1:1-2:4b, which is usually attributed to the P source.

CHAPTER THREE

Appeal to Principles

Overview of the Prophets

The second section of the Hebrew Bible, the Prophets, is traditionally divided into two sections of four books each: Former and Latter. The "Former Prophets" consists of the books of Joshua, Judges, (I and II) Samuel, and (I and II) Kings. They are called "Former" because they come before the next collection of books, that of the "Latter Prophets," which consists of the books of the three "major" prophets, Isaiah, Ezekiel, and Jeremiah, along with the book of the "The Twelve," now divided into separate books for those designated "minor" prophets. (The major prophets get their designation because their books are longer than the others.) In literary style, the Former Prophets are more historical and narrative in nature, as they tell the story of the rise and fall of the Israelite monarchy. This story begins with the conquest of the Promised Land (Joshua), covers the time of the tribal confederacy (Judges), and ends with the monarchy proper (Samuel and Kings). Although the Latter Prophets contain some narrative material, they contain mostly the sermons of the Prophets.

What unites both sections of the Prophets is what can be called the Deuteronomic theology; in fact, the Former Prophets are often referred to as the Deuteronomistic History because they tell the history of the monarchy from the perspective of the Deuteronomic theology.[1] This theology is grounded in Deuteronomy's version of the Covenant at Sinai, which emphasizes, more than Exodus, that obedience to the Law leads to reward and disobedience to punishment. This perspective informs both sections of the Prophets, for the Deuteronomistic history treats the history of ancient Israel as a cycle of disobedience and punishment that leads to the destruction of Jerusalem and the Temple in 587 BCE, followed by the Babylonian Exile.

Put differently, the Prophets tell a story about how the Israelites fail to keep the laws they know and go on to offer a different basis for morality: internalized principles rather than explicit rules. Using the so-called "Two Tables of the Law" (Obligations to God and Obligations to Neighbor) as a guide to our thinking, we will see that both Former and Latter Prophets agree that Israel fails to fulfill both parts of covenant. For simplicity's sake, in what follows I overemphasize how the Former Prophets tend to stress the first Table and the Latter Prophets the second.[2]

The Former Prophets:
The Failure to Love God

The Former Prophets open with the story of the Conquest, as the Israelites are under the leadership of Joshua and encamped to the east of the Jordan River. In the book of Joshua, the Israelites first prepare to enter Canaan (chapters 1-5) and, in a series of campaigns, take control of the land (chapters 6-12). They then divide the land among the twelve tribes (chapters 13-22) and participate in a covenant renewal ceremony in which Joshua reminds the Israelites that their success in the land depends on how well they keep covenant with God (chapters 23-24).

Judges, the next book in the Former Prophets, describes how the Israelites routinely worship other gods and get into trouble. The book takes its name from tribal chieftains upon whom God's spirit periodically rests. God empowers these leaders to deliver the Israelites from the oppression to which God had subjected them for failing to worship God alone. The book describes a repeated cycle of idolatry, oppression, repentance, and deliverance, only for the Israelites to make the same mistake over and over and over again. The story of the first judge, Othniel (3:7-11), serves as a snapshot of the book's plot. The Israelites "do what is offensive to the Lord," which the text identifies as worshipping Canaanite fertility gods and goddesses. God is then said to allow the Israelites to be conquered by their neighbors for eight years. The Israelites cry out, and so God sends Othniel to defeat their enemies. The land rests for forty years, and then the cycle repeats over the careers of eleven other judges, including five major ones: Ehud (3:12-30), Deborah (4:1-5:31), Gideon (6:1-8:32), Jepthah (10:6-12:7), and Samson (13:1-16:31).

The pattern continues into the Monarchy. Saul is anointed the first king of Israel (I Samuel 9) but is rejected by God after he fails to follow God's commands. Interestingly, the biblical texts offer two different stories as to what Saul did to earn God's disfavor. One story, found in I Samuel 13, says that Saul offered sacrifices to God when he was not authorized to do so. The other story, in I Samuel 15, says that Saul failed to obey God's command to kill all the Amalekites and their animals. Either way, Saul fails to do what he knows he should do.

Saul is not the only king who fails to do his duty to God. Solomon, noted for his wisdom, also fails.[3] First Kings 11 tells of the final days of Solomon's reign and attributes his downfall to his idolatry. Solomon, according to the text, had 300 wives and 700 concubines who "turned away his heart" so that he worshiped and encouraged the worship of a number of foreign gods, despite his promises to God to be loyal to him. The result was to be the dissolution of the kingdom after Solomon's death.

The pattern continues during the time of the divided kingdom, as the Deuteronomic historian assesses the reigns of the various kings of Israel and Judah as bad or good by whether they promote the worship of God or allow for the worship of idols or other people's gods. For example, out of fear for his own life, Jereboam, the first king of the northern kingdom of Israel, creates golden calves and declares them to be the god who brought the people out of Egypt (I Kings 12:28-31).[4] Rehoboam, Solomon's son who succeeds his father as king of Judah, the southern kingdom, likewise promotes the worship of other gods (I Kings 14:22-24).

In surveying the accounts of I and II Kings, we discover that only a minority of kings of Judah and Israel were judged to be even somewhat good kings. During the time of the divided monarchy, Israel had 19 kings who reigned for more than a brief period. Of these, only one is judged as a partially good king: Jehu. In II Kings 10:18-29, Jehu slaughters all the worshipers of Baal, thus "eradicating" Baal worship from Israel. He does not, however, repudiate the golden calves set up by Jereboam.

Judah fares a bit better. Of Judah's 19 kings (and one queen) during the era of the divided monarchy, five are considered partially good because they begin to purify worship, although they never complete the task. They are Asa (I Kings 10:15:9-24), Jehosaphat (I Kings 22:41-51), Jehoash (II Kings 12:1-22), Amaziah (II Kings 14:1-22), and Azariah (II Kings 15:1-7). Two more are considered good because they more consistently lead the people to worship the God of Israel alone. The first of these is Hezekiah, who, in the words of the Deuteronomist,

> did what was pleasing to the Lord; just as his father David had done: he abolished the shrines and pillars and cut down the sacred post...He trusted only in the Lord, the God of Israel; there was none like him among all the kings of Judah after him, nor among those before him. He clung to the Lord; he did not turn away from following him, but kept the commandments that the Lord had given to Moses (II Kings 18:3-8).

This is indeed high praise from the Deuteronomist; nonetheless, Hezekiah does make the mistake of showing envoys from Babylon his treasury and armory, thus giving them too much inside intelligence. Isaiah therefore predicts that Babylon will soon invade, to which Hezekiah responds, "Well, at least there is peace in my day" (II Kings 20:12-19). Perhaps he was not a good strategist and a bit shortsighted, but the fact remains that Hezekiah's reign is assessed by the criterion of whether he promotes the worship of God alone. That, at least, he does.

The second good king of Judah is Josiah, whose reign is separated from Hezekiah's by two bad kings, Manasseh and Amon. During Josiah's reign, workers renovating the Temple in Jerusalem discover a scroll of the law, a scroll that many scholars think was the book of Deuteronomy (or at least part of it). When the scroll is shown to Josiah, he initiates wholesale reform of worship and makes Jerusalem the only place for God to be worshiped (II Kings 22:1-23:24a). Thus the author concludes, "... he fulfilled the terms of the Teaching recorded in the scroll ..." and notes that Josiah even outdoes Hezekiah, saying that "there was no king like him before who turned back to the Lord with all his heart and soul and might, in full accord with the Teaching of Moses; nor did any like him arise after him" (II Kings 23:24b-25). Alas, according to the

Deuteronomist, Josiah's reforms were not enough to counterbalance the evil of Manasseh and forestall the Exile (II Kings 23:26-27).

Again, between Israel and Judah, there are a total of 26 kings and 1 queen whose reigns are recorded in I and II Kings. Of the 27, only two are declared unambiguously good—a hit rate of only 5 percent. If we include the five somewhat good kings, we are up to only 23 percent. When one considers that the criteria for assessing whether kings are good or not is whether they promote the exclusive worship of God, then it is clear that the vast majority of times, the kings do not follow the first table of the law.

That love of God is the main concern of the Former Prophets is only reinforced by the Deuteronomist's treatment of King David. After all, David breaks at least three of the commandments from the second table of the Law in his affair with Bathsheba: he covets, commits adultery, and instigates murder. As told in II Samuel 11-12, David sees Bathsheba bathing on a nearby rooftop and sends for her. Even after David finds out that she is married, they have sex and she gets pregnant, which presents David with a problem since Bathsheba's husband, Uriah, is a soldier in David's army and is, at the time of this affair, stationed at the battlefront. David therefore sends for him to come home and take conjugal leave, in the hope that Uriah and Bathsheba will have sex so that Uriah will think that her child is his. Uriah indeed returns to Jerusalem, but loyal soldier that he is, he stays with his own men rather than go home to reconnect with Bathsheba. David then orders that Uriah be put on the front line when he returns to battle. He is and is killed. David does not get away with the affair, however, as Nathan confronts him, leading David to confess his wrongdoing. The unborn child dies, leaving David and Bathsheba to grieve for a time—at least until they have sex again, resulting in the conception of Solomon. Nonetheless, the author does not wholeheartedly condemn David for this and other sins.[5] Why might that be the case?

Earlier in the narrative (II Samuel 7:11b-16), God initiated a covenant with David (often called the Royal, or Davidic, Covenant). In this covenant, God promises that a descendant of David will rule on the throne in Jerusalem forever, regardless of what David's descendants do. This does not mean, however, that they can get away with anything, for God does promise to "discipline" David's descendants; God will not, however, "reject" them as God did with Saul. Aside from giving theological authorization for an Israelite monarchy, the text is surprising because the covenant seems to be unconditional. David seems not to have done anything to deserve this gift; at least nothing is explicitly mentioned here. It could be that David had demonstrated his trust in God many times, such as in his confrontation with and victory over Goliath (I Samuel 17).

We do know, however, that one trait of David is loyalty, even to those who oppose him. After all, David remained loyal to Saul and his household even after their relationship became strained (to put it mildly). This is apparent in David's heartfelt lament over Saul and Jonathan recorded in II Samuel 1:17-27. This poem reads in part:

> Your glory, O Israel/Lies slain on your heights;
> How have the mighty fallen! …
> Saul and Jonathan/Beloved and cherished, …
> Daughters of Israel
> Weep over Saul,
> Who clothed you in crimson and finery,
> Who decked your robes with jewels of gold …

That loyalty may be the key to understanding David becomes apparent when we consider a couple of other assessments. When Samuel delivers the news to Saul that God has rejected him as king of Israel, Samuel tells him that God has chosen someone "after his own heart" to be king (I Samuel 13:14). The someone turns out to be David. Despite whatever faults David might have, he never worships another god. Put differently, he is fiercely loyal to God, just as God is fiercely loyal to Israel. Consider, too, the Deuteronomist's condemnation of Jereboam: "he was not wholehearted with the Lord his God, like his father David" (I Kings 15:4). Whatever his other faults might be, David was 100 percent faithful to God as God was 100 percent faithful to Israel.

To take stock: the Law begins with the commandment to be faithful to the God of the Covenant. The Israelites have been reminded of this and have promised to abide by it (and the rest of the covenant, too, of course) in Joshua, but the books of Judges, Samuel, and Kings tell the story of how the Israelites largely fail to do their proper duty to God, with David as the most notable exception. Again, we see that knowledge of the rules does not guarantee that they will be followed. The Latter Prophets continue this line of thought but shift largely to the so-called second table of the Law to demonstrate how the Israelites fail to do their duties to their neighbors.

The Latter Prophets: Failure to Love Neighbors

The time period covered by the careers of the Latter Prophets spans at least three centuries. Some of these figures preach as early as the eighth century BCE, some during the Exile in the sixth century, and some after that, perhaps as late as the fifth century BCE. While prophecy popularly carries the connotation of "foretelling the future," it is not primarily what the prophetic movement entailed in ancient Israel. Perhaps the best way to understand the prophets is as preachers who call the nations of Israel and Judah to remain faithful to the Covenant. Their criticisms are motivated by a powerful experience of the divine and, to the extent that they address the future, they see events in the near future as actions of God to punish the nations of Israel and/or Judah for failing to keep covenant with God, or as God's action to restore their fortunes after the Exile. For example, Isaiah interprets Cyrus' rise to power and the fall of Babylon as God's action. He identifies Cyrus, Persia's king, as the one whom God has anointed (literally, the messiah) to free the Jewish captives and punish Babylon for being so harsh (see Isaiah 45:1-13 and 47:1-15).

Overall, then, the prophets function as the conscience of the nation in that they are astute critics of the religious, political, and economic status quo. More often than not, the prophets charge Israel and Judah with failing to care for the neighbor, understood as the poor and most vulnerable in society. In doing so, they provide an alternative to a morality based on law—not so much a rejection of law, but a deepening of it.

Consider Amos. Apparently a businessman from Judah, his work took him to the northern Kingdom of Israel, where he witnessed the upper classes exploiting the poor. In his opening oracle against Israel, Amos promises punishment "because they have sold for silver those whose cause was just and the needy for a pair of sandals" (2:6), a charge that is repeated in 8:6. Amos here alludes to loan practices in which people who could not pay their debts became indentured servants. Amos depicts the creditors as being so callous as to enforce this provision of the law to collect small debts. We should also note that Amos condemns the wealthy for bribing judges, the judges who accept those bribes (5:12), and merchants who cheat people by rigging scales and selling less than pure products (8:5b-6).

In response to these outrageous practices, Amos could have charged the people of Israel with breaking specific laws that forbid exploiting the poor and vulnerable, such as those found in Exodus 22:21-24. He could have charged the people with selectively obeying laws, since the text suggests that they are obeying the laws governing worship but neglecting the laws governing human relationships. Instead, he accuses the nation of Israel of violating what we might today call the principle of justice. In a rhetorically powerful section, Amos reports that God "hates" the religious festivals that the people keep faithfully and rejects their offerings and songs—the very things that God had commanded them to do in the Law! Instead of being liturgically faithful, Amos declares that God wants the people to "let justice well up like water and righteousness like an unfailing stream" (5:24). Justice and righteousness function here as parallel terms indicating that people should simply "do right by others," as those of us in the South might say.[6]

Lest we leave the impression that only the northern kingdom of Israel was guilty of exploiting the vulnerable, Isaiah and Micah charge Judah with the same crimes and likewise call the people to justice. Isaiah, speaking to Judah at the same point in history as Amos preaches in Israel, accuses the people of "grinding the face of the poor" (3:17) and promises vengeance on the wealthy for taking bribes (5:7-24), even comparing them to Sodom and Gomorrah. Isaiah also predicts judgment unless the people "learn to do good, seek justice, rescue the oppressed, defend the orphan, plead for the widow" (1:17). Micah, like Isaiah, speaks to the perceived corruption of Judah and in his sermon recreates a courtroom scene (6:6-8). He begins by asking, "With what shall I come to the Lord" and lists a variety of offerings one might bring. He then answers by saying that God has already told us what is good, i.e., to "do justice, and to love kindness, and to walk humbly with your God." In sum, we see that a theme that runs consistently through the sermons of eighth-century prophets is that knowledge of the law is not enough to stem the tide of destructive behaviors. Instead, they suggest that a better foundation for morality consists of abstract principles such as justice and righteousness.

Implied in these calls to act on principle is a different locus for moral motivation. Whereas motivation for following the law comes from outside the person—in the form of rewards and punishments—these principles are to be internalized so that the motivation for heeding them will come from within. Put differently, the motivation for being just, for example, comes from making principles part of our identities. This at least seems to be the moral force of Jeremiah's account of a new covenant in Jeremiah 31: 33, where God says that the new covenant will be "put into their inmost being" and carved "upon their hearts."

So how does this attempt to change the focus of morality by the eighth-century prophets fare? Amos, Isaiah, and Micah preach before Assyria conquers Israel and Babylon takes the people of Judah into Exile. Do the people learn from those experiences and heed the prophets? It would appear not, for later prophets deliver similar messages. Take Jeremiah in the sixth century, writing to Judah after the Assyrian conquest of Israel and shortly before the Babylonian invasion of Judah. Jeremiah promises punishment for those who grow "fat and sleek" by exploiting others and failing to care justly for the poor (5:28). Jeremiah also reminds Josiah's son that his father did well when he "ate and drank and dispensed justice with righteousness" (22:15). Jeremiah goes on to accuse the present generation of "dishonest gain" and "shedding innocent blood, and for practicing oppression and violence" (22:17).

What about after the Exile? Most scholars date the last few chapters of Isaiah to late in the sixth century or early in the fifth, after Persia has conquered Babylon and the Jewish people have been allowed to go home to rebuild their lives. The author/preacher of Isaiah 58 continues to decry ritual allegiance that is uncoupled from justice. Speaking of the practice of fasting, he accuses the people of fasting for selfish reasons and says that the fast that God wants is "to loose the bonds of injustice, to undo the thongs of the yoke, to let the oppressed go free" and to "share your bread with the hungry and bring the homeless poor into your house; when you see the naked to cover them, and not to hide yourself from your own kin?" (Isaiah 58:6-7). Later, the prophet says that God was displeased that there was no justice (59:16) and calls for a new Jubilee that will allow the poor to start over (61:1-2).[7]

Taken together, then, both Former and Latter Prophets suggest that a morality built around following explicit rules is problematic. Both develop what was foreshadowed in certain parts of the Law, i.e., that simply knowing the laws is not enough to guarantee that people will follow them, whether the laws govern relation to God or others. The Latter Prophets dig deeper into the laws and suggest that the laws point us to principles of justice and righteousness that should become such a part of our identity or character that they guide our actions. That this message, first spoken in the eighth century, does not seem to have gotten through

Does God Keep the Law?

We have seen that knowledge of the law does not guarantee that people will keep the Law. What about God? Recall that we said earlier that God, as a character in the story of the Torah, seems to need guidelines as much as human beings. Does God fare any better than us in the Prophets?

On the one hand, God seems to be very good at keeping the promise to protect Israel when it keeps the Covenant and punishing the people when they do not. We have seen this pattern is the plot of the book of Judges. Moreover, we have seen how the Prophets, both Former and Latter, suggest that the Exile is God's punishment for breaking both Tables of the Law.

On the other hand, there are still times when God seems to ignore the Law. In II Samuel 6, David decides to bring the Ark to Jerusalem. David's soldiers load it onto an ox-drawn cart and proceed to Jerusalem. At one point along the way the oxen stumble, threatening to spill the Ark onto the ground. Uzzah reaches out to steady it and "grasps" the Ark. At that point, God becomes "incensed" at Uzzah's "indiscretion" and kills Uzzah. Is this not murder, or at least manslaughter? (See Exodus 21:12-13 for an example of the distinction.) While it is true that people were enjoined not to touch holy objects unless they wanted to die (Numbers 4:15), the text attributes God's action to intense anger, not to issuing a just punishment for violating a divine command.

to later generations suggests that building morality around internalized principles was no more successful than building morality around laws. Is there another option? Yes, but we first need to engage the Writings.

Questions for Discussion

1. The Former Prophets can be compared to an argument by example. The thesis is that God rewards faithfulness to the Covenant and punishes unfaithfulness. The narrative contains example after example of situations in which this is the case, some of which were identified in this chapter. Are you convinced by the argument made in the Former Prophets? Why or why not? Consider not only biblical examples, but also examples from everyday life—even your own.

2. Look more closely at the following episodes in David's life. Which actions would you call wise? Foolish? Explain why.

    •   David and Goliath: I Samuel 17

    •   David spares the life of Saul, who is trying to kill him: I Samuel 24 and 26

- David dances as the Ark is brought into Jerusalem, causing a rift between him and one of his wives, Michal: II Samuel 6

- David fails to act when his daughter, Tamar, is raped by her half-brother, Amnon: II Samuel 13.

- David does what he knows is wrong in taking a census, even though the text says that God "incited" him to do it. He asks God what he should do for penance and is given three choices: II Samuel 25.

- Looking at David's life as a whole, how wise would you say he was? Explain.

3. Consider the biblical account of Josiah. We have seen that he is considered a good king because he purifies the worship of God. Read II Kings 23:4-25 to see how violently he went about ensuring that God alone was worshiped—including killing priests and burning their bones on various altars. How wise do you think these actions were? Explain. Does that change our assessment of Josiah as a good king? Should it?

4. Consider the opposition with which the prophet's messages are often met. See, for example, Amos 7:10-13 and Jeremiah 20:1-2, 26:1-11, and 38:1-6. Is it wise to confront power? Explain.

5. Consider the appeals to justice, righteousness, and mercy found in the sermons of the Latter Prophets. Do you find those principles more or less helpful than rules in determining what to do? Explain.

6. Consider Jeremiah's advice to the Exiles in Jeremiah 29:4-14. Do you think this is wise advice? Explain.

Endnotes

[1]Biblical scholars disagree on the history of the Deuteronomic writings, although the writings are often traced to the religious reforms initiated by Josiah, king of Judah from 640-609 BCE, whose story can be found in II Kings 22:1-23:30. The consensus about the Deuteronomistic history, such as it is, is that a version existed prior to the Babylonian Exile and that it was reworked during or after the Exile, in part to explain that the Exile was God's punishment for failing to keep the covenant.

[2]The keyword here is "tend," for close reading of the Prophets suggests that this division is overly simplistic. Just one example of how the Former Prophets show a concern for injustices can be found in the story of Elijah's condemnation of Ahab and Jezebel for killing Naboth so as to seize his vineyard in I Kings 21. A single example of how the Latter Prophets show concern for worshiping God rightly can be found in Hosea, who uses the metaphor of an unfaithful spouse to describe Israel's proclivity to worship other gods (see, for example, 2:16-18). Regardless of the oversimplification, it is still true that Former and Latter Prophets agree that the Israelites fail to keep either Table of the Law.

[3]I will say more later about David, Saul's successor and Solomon's father.

[4]Whether the calves were actually idols or simply served as pedestals for the throne of the invisible YHWH is a matter of interpretive debate. Regardless, Jereboam decentralizes the worship of God by erecting altars at Dan and Bethel, thus violating Deuteronomistic laws and potentially opening the door to idolatry.

[5]For David's other failures as a parent and a king, see II Samuel 9-20 and I Kings 1-2.

[6]James Luther May, *Amos*, The Old Testament Library (Philadelphia: The Westminster Press, 1969), 91-93.

[7]The law of Jubilee can be found in Leviticus 25 and allows for debts to be canceled and people to return to any ancestral lands that they may have had to sell because of debt. As best we can tell, the law was never practiced, at least in full, but it would have functioned as a way to break the cycle of poverty so that each generation had a chance to make a fresh start.

CHAPTER FOUR

Conflicting Advice for Living in a Hard, Cruel World

Overview of the Writings

The third section of the Hebrew canon, the Writings, is widely recognized as the most diverse portion of the canon. It contains an array of genres, including poetry (Psalms and Song of Songs), short stories (Ruth and Esther), wisdom (Proverbs, Job, and Ecclesiastes), and history (I and II Chronicles). These different literary genres reflect such different perspectives that we do not see in the Writings the thematic and chronological unity that we find in the Law and the Prophets. In fact, the books seem to represent a variety of sentiments that do not always cohere with the Law and Prophets.

As the last section of the TNK to be canonized, many of these texts were written in a post-exilic world. (Recall Chapter One for a discussion of the social, political, and theological crises of the Exile.) At this point in their history, it would seem that at least some of the ancient Jewish people had come to perceive that this is a hard, cruel world in which being God's people is not what they thought it would be, and God is not who they thought God would be.[1] As I try imaginatively to enter into the world of readers living at this time, I have come to see this collection of literature as representative of debates in ancient Israel over how one should live in such a world. Consider the Writings to reflect the "culture wars" of post-Exilic Judaism. To make the case, we will examine three areas of debate found in the Writings: how to relate to God, how to relate to foreigners, and how to respond to our enemies.

Psalms and Job:
Competing Views of How to Relate to God

The Psalms and Job offer contrasting ways of relating to a God who has put people through an event as traumatic as Exile. Here I focus on laments, those psalms that give voice to the anguish of those who suffer. The laments provide examples of individuals and communities who hold God accountable to keep God's commitments and to act like God. For example, Psalm 22 is an individual lament in which the speaker feels abandoned by God. To get a response from God, the psalmist obliquely asserts his own virtue by continuing to acknowledge the holiness of God (22:3), reminds God that God has cared for both the ancestors and him in the past (22:4-5, 9-10), and promises to tell others of God's deliverance should God, in fact, deliver him (22:22-24). In short, the author argues that God should rescue him because (1) that is what God has done in the past, (2) God has invested a lot already in his life, and (3) God will get a lot of good publicity if the psalmist is delivered.

Consider as well the communal lament of Psalm 74, which reflects the aftermath of the destruction of the Temple in Jerusalem by the Babylonians. The psalmist admits to feeling abandoned by God (74:1), reminds God of how the Babylonians desecrated the Temple (74:4-10) and laughed at God (74:11, 18, 22-23), reminds God of the power exhibited at creation (74:12-17), and calls God to honor the covenant (74:20). Put differently, the psalmist makes the case that God should rescue them because (1) God's reputation is being impugned, (2) God has the power to act, and (3) God has obligated Godself to act on their behalf because of the covenant.

By attending to the argumentative pattern imbedded in the laments, we see that the authors appeal to God to save them on a number of grounds, many of which we have seen here. Although it may seem impious to readers today to think that God must be persuaded to do the right thing, this is not a new trope in ancient Judaism, for it permeates some of the oldest layers of the tradition. Abraham tries to persuade God not to destroy Sodom and Gomorrah (Genesis 19). Moses persuades God not to wipe out the Israelites for making the golden calf right after ratifying the covenant at Sinai (Exodus 32). In a world in which the Jewish people have been disappointed and disheartened by events that strike at the heart of their religious and national identities, the laments say that we should hold God accountable for doing the right thing.

In contrast to the laments, the book of Job seems to encourage readers to walk away from God—a reading I acknowledge to be provocative. According to most biblical scholars, the book is likely an adaptation of earlier folk tales and was written around the time of the Exile. Against this historical background, it is plausible to read the book of Job as a voice of protest against those who say that the ancient Israelites should remain loyal to God, even after unspeakable tragedy. Let me be clear, too, that I am not advocating that readers follow the path that I contend Job takes as a character in the story. Instead, I simply wish to register that given a post-Exilic readership for the book, it is not unreasonable to assume that at least some people want to be done with God. The book falls into three distinct sections: a prose prologue (Chapters 1-2), a poetic core that consists of a series of speeches that climax with a confrontation between Job and God (Chapters 3:1-42:6), and a prose conclusion that tries to wrap up the story (and the key word here is "tries").

To make a long story too short, Job is sincerely devoted to God and blessed with wealth and a large family. Unbeknown to him, God and the Satan decide to test him to see if his faith is real or just a matter of convenience.[2] Two sets of disasters befall Job, but both times, he verbalizes a striking confession of faith: "the Lord has given, and the Lord has taken away; blessed be the name of the Lord" (Job 1:21) and "Should we accept only good from God and not accept evil?" (Job 2:10b). As the story continues, three friends come and sit with Job in silence. Job then curses the day he was born, after which the friends try to explain to him that he is suffering because he has done something wrong. As the speeches continue, Job becomes increasingly impatient with his friends, protests his innocence, accuses God of not playing fair, and demands to speak to God—even if he has no hope of getting justice from the encounter. The friends continue to defend God's reputation, which only makes Job escalate, which only makes them escalate, with the result that all are caught in a downward spiral of accusations and protests. After the third cycle of speeches, the effect of which is to leave the reader increasingly hopeless that the debate can be resolved, a fourth person chimes in, but adds little new to the debate. God has still not shown up to right the situation. Yet.

Finally, in chapters 38-41, God appears and says, in effect, "Who do you think you are? You have been demanding answers from me, little man. Well, before I answer you, maybe you can answer some questions for me!" God then launches into a series of rhetorical questions in which God harangues Job by asking if Job can create the universe or control Leviathan and Behemoth, which are ancient symbols of chaos and disorder. Of course, Job cannot do these things, and all God's speech establishes is that God is stronger than Job. But God's reply misses Job's point, for Job has been complaining that God is not fair, not that God is too weak to bring his torture to an end. As Miles characterizes God's response to Job, God "hides...by rising to his full majestic stature, drawing the robes of creation around him, and regally changing the subject" from God's justice to God's power.[3] Job, however, gets the last word when he says, in essence,

> I already know, God, that you are all-powerful. Your power is not the issue, your justice is! Yes, I have spoken about things of which I know nothing—your character. I thought I knew who you were, but now that I have seen you for what you really are, I give up the fight, recant my beliefs in your goodness, and fear for the fate of all mortal flesh (Job 42:1-6).

In some translations, Job says that he despises himself and repents, but this translation is problematic for several reasons. I mention two.[4] First, Job has done nothing for which he needs to repent. Second, God never reveals a secret sin that Job has committed such that he deserves all that has befallen him. In effect, what Job has done in this speech is to expose God as all-powerful, but not loving.

In the epilogue, God gets angry at Job's friends because they have lied about him (Job 42:7)—a striking admission, because throughout the book they have been defending God's goodness and justice! For God to say that they are lying means that God confesses, albeit obliquely, that God is *not*, in fact, fair or just! After Job prays for his friends, God restores Job's fortunes twice over and grants him more children. Thereafter, Job lives a long life and dies "old and contented" (42:16-17)—without apparently addressing God again. Job does not offer a confession of faith at this point, as he did earlier. Job does not say, "the Lord gives, the Lord takes, the Lord gives again, blessed be the name of the Lord" or the like at the end of the story. Instead, the author depicts Job living happily ever after with his family. We can therefore infer that Job is done with God and has walked away. I know I am making much of silence here, but to me the silence veritably shouts.

It is hard, I recognize, to read Job in this way, but given the post-Exilic time in which it was written, who can blame people for wanting to be done with God? That this is a plausible response is only reinforced by some of the post-Holocaust literature of the late 20th century in which some writers say they are done with God.[5] People whose hopes and identities have been dashed by events that crash down upon them can hardly be blamed for wanting to walk away from God. There is much more that could be said about this topic of suffering, but for our purposes, we should note that the Writings offer at least two conflicting bits of advice on how to relate to God in a hard, cruel world. The laments encourage

How Does the Book of Job Explain Innocent Suffering?

One of the intriguing issues that scholars debate is whether the prose sections are original to the story or later additions to the poetic core. One reason for the debate is that the different sections of the text provide different answers to the question, "Why do bad things happen to good people?" According to the prologue, the answer to why the innocent Job suffers is simple: God is testing the integrity of his faith. In the poetic core of the book, neither the friends nor God reveal any "smoking gun" that proves Job's guilt—all of which would seem to deconstruct the punitive view of suffering, without offering any alternative. Then God, in his speeches, says that bad things happen to good people because God has created a world that includes chaos and disorder. Finally, in the epilogue, God ends up restoring Job's fortunes, which makes it seem that God rewards Job for enduring the test. If this is the case, then does the author intend to rehabilitate the punitive notion of suffering? In the end, does the book really offer an answer to the question of why the innocent suffer?

readers to hold God accountable to act as God should, and the book of Job encourages readers to be done with God, get on with their lives, and enjoy their families.

Ezra and Ruth:
Conflicting Advice on How to Relate to Foreigners

As noted in Chapter One, in 538 BCE, Cyrus of Persia issues an Edict of Restoration that allows the Jewish people to return to Judah. (Versions of the edict can be found in Ezra 1:1-4 and 6:1-5, as well as II Chronicles 36:22-23.) Over time, a number of Jewish people return to set up life again in Judah, which is now a province of the Persian Empire consisting of Jerusalem and a small part of the surrounding territory. In the biblical narrative, Ezra is the Jewish priest who is responsible for rebuilding Judaism and bringing the Law with him from Babylon, while Nehemiah is the governor responsible for the rebuilding of the city of Jerusalem. As the book of Ezra tells the story, Ezra returns and discovers that "the people of Israel and the priests and the Levites have not separated themselves from the peoples of the land whose abhorrent practices are like those of the Canaanites…" (Ezra 9:1). Ezra goes into mourning and eventually says that the Israelites can be saved if they "expel all these women and those who have been born to them," which all Israel agrees to do (Ezra 10:4-5). The allusion to Canaan is instructive here because it echoes the story of the Conquest and the view found in the former prophets, i.e., that the Exile happened because the Israelites did not separate themselves from others and therefore kept worshiping the gods of those people. In short, Ezra wants to make sure Exile does not happen again and so encourages the men to divorce any foreign wives and thus abandon their families. Ezra, for the sake of the survival of Judah, insists on maintaining ethnic purity.

The short story of Ruth contrasts with Ezra's view of foreigners. Ruth's story is set during the time of the judges, but scholars debate when it was written. Some date it to the time of the united monarchy and see it as a celebration of Davidic rule. Others argue that it was written as late as 500 BCE, when it would serve as a counterpoint to Ezra. Regardless of when the book was written, in a post-Exilic context the story raises questions about Ezra's worry about foreigners because it makes the central figure—and heroine—a foreign woman. And not just any foreigner, but a Moabite (see below).

According to the story, Elimelech, his wife Naomi, and their two sons leave the Promised Land because of famine and take up residence in Moab. The sons marry Moabite women, Orpah and Ruth. All goes well until all three husbands die, leaving Naomi and her daughters-in-law as widows. Naomi decides to return home, so both Orpah and Ruth decide to go with her. Naomi tries to deter them. She dissuades Orpah, but Ruth insists on accompanying her back to Israel, making a well-known pledge that "wherever you go, I will go, wherever you lodge, I will lodge; your people will be my people and your God will be my God" (Ruth 1:16). Naomi relents, and once they return home, Ruth and Naomi conspire to get Boaz, a distant kinsman, to marry Ruth, thus providing economic security for the two widows. It works, and the story ends with Ruth giving birth to Obed, who is said to become the grandfather of David, who will go on to become king of Israel.

In short, a foreign woman is the vessel through which Israel's glorious future comes to be. But the story becomes even more intriguing because Ruth is a Moabite. According to Genesis 19, the Moabites were the descendants of Lot's incestuous relationship with his daughters. They also failed to show hospitality to the Israelites during their wanderings in the wilderness (Numbers 22-24). Because of this history of animosity, the Moabites (along with the Ammonites) were not to be allowed to join the "congregation" of the Israelites (Deuteronomy 23:4-5). Later in the canonical sequence, the Moabites oppressed the Israelites (Judges 3). The Moabites were not, therefore, well-liked—or considered trustworthy. The book of Ruth gives no hint of this animosity, however, and says, in effect, that the Israelites should not do what Ezra says. In a post-Exilic context, the book of Ruth thus celebrates ethnic intermarriage and suggests that foreigners can bring blessings to the people of Israel.

Esther and Daniel:
Conflicting Advice on How to Respond to Enemies

Esther and Daniel both reflect the tensions between Jews and Greeks, and so I begin with a brief summary of the Greek era of post-Exilic Jewish life. In 333 BCE, Alexander the Great conquers Palestine. After his death in 326 BCE, his generals—the most important of whom, for purposes of the biblical stories, are Ptolemy and Seleucus—vie for control of the Empire. Seleucus comes to rule Judea, and one of his descendants, Antiochus IV, rules from 175-163 BCE. He was also known as Epiphanes—a term we will see is significant. Antiochus IV actively persecuted the Jewish people by raiding the Temple treasury and even outlawing the practice of Judaism. Not only that, he claimed to be a manifestation of God (which is what "Epiphanes" means). In 167 BCE, he enters the Temple, sets up an altar to Zeus in the Holy of Holies (the inner-most part of the Temple, where God's presence was said to abide), and sacrifices a pig. This and Antiochus' other actions spur the Maccabean revolt (see I Maccabees 1-2). It is Antiochus IV's reign that seems to be the historical backdrop for both the books of Esther and Daniel.[6]

Esther, like Ruth, is a short story, although it is perhaps better classified as a farce because of its comic portrayal of many of the persons in the story and the many improbable turns of events. The story is set during the time of the Persian Empire and tells of a young Jewish woman who saves her people from a plan to exterminate them. The story begins when Vashti, Queen of Persia, finds herself divorced for failing to obey the king's command to dance—arguably nude—in front of a bunch of drunk men. The king stages what amounts to a beauty pageant to find the next queen, a contest which all young women are compelled to enter and one that Esther happens to win. On another front, the king's advisor, Haman, becomes incensed that Esther's uncle, Mordecai, refuses to honor him, and so Haman plots to exterminate the Jews. He manipulates the king, who does not know that Esther is Jewish, into issuing an edict calling Persians to kill all Jews on a certain date. Mordecai learns of the plot, informs Esther, and encourages her to use her position as queen to save her people. She exposes the plot, Haman is killed, and she convinces the king to issue a new edict allowing the Jewish people to defend themselves. As the book reaches its climax, the Jewish people slaughter those who would have killed them (more than 75,000, according to the text) and throw a party. As the book ends, Esther remains queen and Mordecai, who had earlier foiled an assassination plot against the king, ends up as the king's chief advisor.

One other important fact about this story is that God is never mentioned.[7] At no point do any of the characters address God or seek God's help. At no point does the narrator tell us that God acts behind the scenes to orchestrate events in such a way as to save God's people. God is not only silent; God is absent from the narrative. The book of Esther thus depicts a world in which the ruling powers are out to persecute, if not exterminate, the Jewish people. In such a world, Esther and Mordecai model those who—on their own, without seeking or receiving assistance from God—outwit their enemies and use lethal force to protect themselves. Put differently, they engage in a preemptive strike and "do unto others" *before* it is done unto them. If readers of the story identify with the characters, then the book will have the effect of encouraging readers to act like the central characters of the story, which in this case means developing the confidence in one's ability to outwit one's enemies and use force to defeat them.

The book of Daniel counsels a different response to enemies, one of civil disobedience that is born of a trust in God. Like Esther, the book is set in a historical era before the time it was actually written. It begins with the Babylonian Exile. Daniel is depicted as one of the members of the leadership elite to be deported to Babylon, where he is asked to do things that violate his religious faith. He is told to eat things that Jewish dietary law forbids. He makes a deal with his guards to let him follow his diet and see how well he does. As the text puts it, "When the ten days were over, they [he and his friends] looked better and healthier than all the youths who were eating the king's food" (Daniel 1:15). Later in the book (Daniel 3), the king issues an edict that commands people to worship a statue. Daniel's three friends, remembering the first commandment, refuse to worship the idol and are thrown into a furnace, where, instead of being cremated, they are protected by an angel. Still later in the book (now set during the reign of Persian king Darius), the king issues an edict banning the worship of anyone but him. Daniel, of course, refuses to do so and is thrown into a pit of lions, where he is again protected (Daniel 6).

In short, when one's enemies seek to prevent one from following the faith, Daniel serves as an example of someone who refuses to capitulate. Instead, he remains faithful to God, disobeys the rulers, accepts their punishments, and is protected from harm. He is a model of non-violent civil disobedience—a stark contrast to those who, like Esther, would seek to respond to threats by means of lethal force.

Looking Back, Looking Ahead

We see that the Writings immerse us into what appear to be debates among the ancient Israelites about how to live in a post-Exilic world, one in which Israel would never, foreseeably at least, exist again as an independent nation. Instead, the Jewish people would be subject to the successive empires of the Persians, Greeks, and Romans. In facing such a world, the Writings embody debates on a number of issues. In relation to God, do we hold God accountable or do we walk away and seek solace in our family? When confronted with foreigners, do we perceive them as threat or as family? When enemies challenge us, do we take up the sword and fight or practice civil disobedience and trust in God to deliver us?

To which set of voices should readers listen and heed? Perhaps now we are ready to hear wisdom calling out in the midst of the cacophony. In the next chapter, we will turn our attention to understanding wisdom's place in the TNK. We will begin with a look at the personification of wisdom in Proverbs, a book that is located early in the Writings (only Psalms comes before it). We will then explore, in more detail, wisdom in the Jewish tradition and its similarities and differences with other ancient wisdom, as well as current work in the psychology of wisdom.

Questions for Discussion

1. Scholars have long noted similarities between the characters of Joseph (from Genesis 37-50) and Daniel. Both are portrayed as Jewish people who rise to positions of power in foreign empires, in large part because of their abilities to interpret dreams. Both are also often described as paradigms or exemplars of wisdom. Look at their stories again in more detail. How else are they alike? How are they different? Does one seem wiser than the other? Why?

2. Consider the story of Esther, in which the Jewish people outwit the plot to exterminate them. Are Esther and Mordecai wise or merely clever? Is there a difference between wisdom and cleverness? Explain.

3. As we have seen, the Writings offer readers conflicting advice about how to live in a hard, cruel world. When have you been faced with conflicting advice on how to deal with a problem? How did you decide? In retrospect, would you call those decisions wise? Why or why not?

4. In the Writings, readers are asked most explicitly to enter a post-Exilic world, since many of the books of the Writings were written during or after the Exile. Review the description of the post-Exilic world from chapter one and your answer to discussion question 4 there. How would you change your answer, if at all? What do you now see as the most important similarities and differences?

Endnotes

[1]Of course, to say this is not to say that earlier generations of readers would have thought life was easy. Clearly the ancient Jewish people had experienced extreme hardship earlier in their history, as in Egypt. The Exile, however, seems to have been a tipping point that galvanized significant dissent from religious authorities.

[2]"Satan" is here not a proper name, but "the Satan," a title of a functionary—literally, the adversary—who is depicted in this story as part of God's heavenly court, a loyal servant who functions something like a prosecuting attorney. The Satan's job appears to be that of poking and prodding God's creation to see that it is what it is supposed to be. We might reasonably understand the Satan as God's quality assurance manager.

[3]Jack Miles, *God: A Biography*. (New York, Vintage Books, 1995), 315. Miles also compares God to a cornered politician (321).

[4]For more on the intricacies of the Hebrew of Job's speech in 42:1-6, see Miles (318-327) and Leo G. Perdue, *Wisdom Literature: A Theological History* (Louisville: Westminster John Knox Press, 2007), 122-126.

[5]See, for example, David R. Blumenthal, *Facing the Abusing God* (Louisville: Westminster John Knox, 1993), 252-253. The temptation to leave religion because of the experience of extreme suffering is not just a Jewish phenomenon, for the problem of innocent suffering has become the main justification for atheism in the modern world. See Kenneth Surin, *Theology and the Problem of Evil* (New York: Basil Blackwell, Inc., 1986), 9.

[6]Scholars agree more that this is the time that Daniel was written than they do about Esther. I side with a few who give this late date to Esther since it reflects the tensions that fit the Greek era, not the Persian era in which the story is set.

[7]This is true at least in the version of the story found in the Hebrew Bible. The *Septuagint*, a translation of the Hebrew Bible plus the Apocrypha into Greek, contains a different version of the story in which God is mentioned multiple times. God's providence is affirmed, as are God's laws, and God is said to intervene at least once in affairs. Scholars have reached no consensus about how to explain these differences. It is possible that the Greek portions of the text were part of the original text and later dropped from the Hebrew version. It is also possible that they were later additions intended to make the book more palatable to orthodox audiences. In the first century CE, rabbis wanted to exclude the book, but it was too popular.

CHAPTER 5

Wisdom Calls

We have been engaged in a thought experiment by reading the Old Testament with a particular question in mind: "What can we learn from it about moral development?" In doing so, we have largely bracketed out the historical world behind the text, except for suggesting that the TNK, on the whole, reflects the experiences of post-Exilic Judaism. We have read the Old Testament in the order of books as found in the Hebrew canon—that is, as literature that tells a story that shapes the identity of a religious community. We have also read the texts naively to keep from imposing too many of our preexisting ideas onto the text and therefore obscuring facets of the story.

In reading these texts in this way, we have seen that the Law tells a story of the need for order that results in the development of explicit guidelines so that God and humanity know how to act in relationship to one another. Even in the Law, however, we see hints that slavishly following rules will not work out well. The Prophets rub our noses in those failures and then respond by substituting appeals to internalized principles, such as justice, in place of laws. The Writings reflect debates that call into question both Law and Prophets as the authors give conflicting advice on how to live in a hard, cruel world. The TNK thus would seem to conclude on a cacophony of discordant notes.

However, if we look (or listen) closely, we hear a voice that may give us some direction. At the beginning of Chapter One, we defined wisdom as the ability to discern the course of action that will lead to the most good that can be achieved in a particular set of circumstances. Now it is time to look more deeply into wisdom. We begin with the call of Lady Wisdom in Proverbs, set out what wisdom means in the context of ancient Judaism, explore the implications of extra-canonical developments in the relationship of wisdom to Law, and conclude with some exercises intended to set us on the road to wisdom.

Lady Wisdom

We meet Lady Wisdom in Proverbs, a book that, in the canonical order of the Writings, comes after Psalms but before readers are immersed deeply into the conflicting views to be found in the rest of this section of the Writings. Lady Wisdom's words thus serve as an apt introduction to what is to follow: an invitation to seek wisdom as we engage the conflicting voices around us. Lady Wisdom appears in both Proverbs 1 and Proverbs 8-9, at the beginning and the conclusion of the first section of the book. In Proverbs 1, wisdom is personified as a prophetess who warns people of the costs of folly. In chapter 8, she calls out to everyone within range of her voice, asserts that her ways are just, promises rewards to those who come to learn from her, and establishes her credibility by saying that she was the first-born of all creation, a co-creator with God.[1] In chapter 9, Lady Wisdom takes on the role of a hostess who has prepared a banquet and invites all to partake. Her feast, she asserts, will fill the soul, unlike those who are seduced by the food and manner of "Lady Folly." But what is wisdom?

Wisdom in Ancient Israel

In ancient Israel, wisdom is often associated with the institutions of family, the Royal Court, and Schools. Later, the sages—teachers of wisdom—are associated with the Scribes and Rabbis.[2] Thus wisdom has to do with the education of the young, as well as the task of governing the nation. As such, the term wisdom (*chochmah*) has many layers of meaning.[3] Among them are practical skills in creating works of art, as well as adeptness or competence in a task. Wisdom can also refer to the ability to address people and circumstances in a way that effectively promotes the living of a meaningful life. Wisdom therefore presupposes some idea of what is good or meaningful, whether the good refers to a piece of art or a life well-lived. (We will explore a more robust notion of this good below.) Thus, *chochmah* should be taken in a holistic, expansive way. As Brown puts it, wisdom is "more than knowledge, more than ability, more than skill or expertise. It is all of the above and then some: it captures the sum and substance of 'virtue-osity.'"[4] Building on these matters, I take wisdom in the Hebrew Bible to refer *at the very least* to the skills needed to discern which voices to listen to and which paths to follow to live a good life.

However, this meaning contracts a bit when the TNK is translated into Greek, where *chochmah* is translated as *sophia*, a term that in ancient Greek refers to the ability to discover what is ultimately real, eternal, and true via our powers of reason and intelligence.[5] Perhaps this is a good reminder that no translation is perfect, for *chochmah* seems to be a much richer term that also includes what the Greeks would have called *techne* (technical skill) and *phronesis* (practical wisdom). I therefore follow Paul Fiddes, who sees *chochmah* as the integration of *phronesis* and *sophia*, such that practical judgments about how to act are guided by a vision of final reality.[6]

To gain further clarity on wisdom, I want to put it into conversation with Aristotle's account of moral development, for he is something of the poster child for our understanding of *phronesis* in the ancient West (see the chart on the next page).[7] For Aristotle, *phronesis* is the central virtue, or excellence, in his account of ethics. It connects the intellectual virtues (including *sophia*) that help us to think well with the moral virtues that help us to desire what is good in healthy ways. We might therefore think of *phronesis* as the conductor of the ensemble of human capacities for thinking, feeling, and choosing—or, to shift metaphors, the keystone that holds all the other pieces of the arch together, or a bridge that connects reason and desire. Practical wisdom involves discriminating discernment of the details of a situation so that we can act in such a way as to attain the most good possible under the circumstance. Aristotle calls this good *eudaimonia*, which means an authentically human flourishing in community with others. Put succinctly, then, for Aristotle the practically wise person can discern the particulars of a situation so as to act in ways that achieve the most of an authentically human good attainable at the time. Practical reasoning thus unites good thinking with appropriate desire in the service of the good. Wisdom is learned, according to Aristotle, by extensive, coached practice in imitating people who are wise. The end result of such practice is that the deliberations of the practically

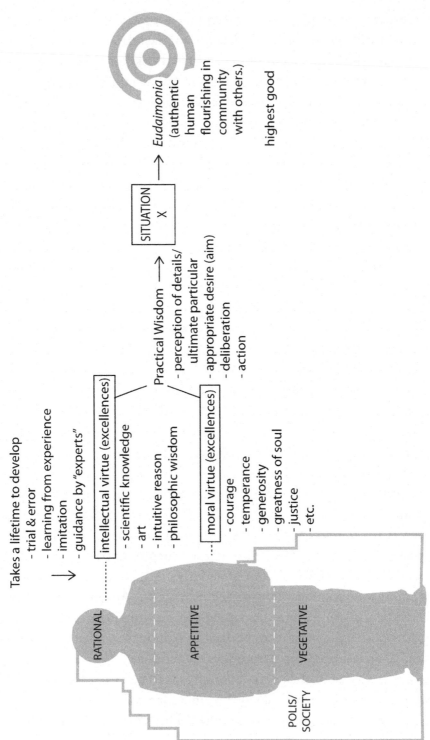

Takes a lifetime to develop
 - trial & error
 - learning from experience
 - imitation
 - guidance by "experts"

→

RATIONAL

intellectual virtue (excellences)
 - scientific knowledge
 - art
 - intuitive reason
 - philosophic wisdom

moral virtue (excellences)
 - courage
 - temperance
 - generosity
 - greatness of soul
 - justice
 - etc.

APPETITIVE

VEGETATIVE

POLIS/
SOCIETY

Person in
Society

Practical Wisdom →
 - perception of details/
   ultimate particular
 - appropriate desire (aim)
 - deliberation
 - action

SITUATION
X

Eudaimonia
(authentic
human
flourishing in
community
with others.)

highest good

wise person may appear automatic to observers because the process has become so deeply internalized that it becomes "second nature," just as the performance of a star athlete or musician can seem so effortless that we forget how much drudgery and practice it takes to get to that point.

This comparison of Hebrew and Greek notions of wisdom raises some important questions. How do we develop wisdom? Does ancient Judaism have an equivalent notion to Aristotle's *eudaimonia*? Does *chokmah* mean that rules and principles are of no use in living ethically? We will take each of these questions in turn.

As to how one becomes wise, we quickly discover that nowhere in Proverbs does Lady Wisdom tell us explicitly how to develop this virtue. There are clues, however, for those with eyes to see. The first is that we are told that wisdom begins with the fear of the Lord.[8] Here, fear is best understood as an awe and reverence for God that motivates or energizes us to action, although it does not rule out some hint of what we normally think of as fear, as the things that attract us often also evoke some degree of fear such that we want to keep our distance from them while being attracted to them.[9] Think of the people who chase after tornadoes, whether for the thrill of it or for legitimate purposes of learning more about the power of these storms. They are both attracted to and wary of the storms.

The hint that wisdom begins with the fear of God may not give us explicit guidance, but it does provide a provocative starting point for understanding wisdom. Consider fear. Since it is an emotional/motivational response to something, wisdom entails developing the desires or motivational structure that enable one to discern and act on the good. Now, consider God. At the very least, God is something bigger than ourselves, something beyond our abilities to shape and control, something that evokes a deep and abiding sense of awe and reverence. Thus we begin to develop wisdom when we decenter our individual selves—arguably even humanity as a species, if God's speech to Job is right—in the service of something bigger than our own well-being, of a more inclusive cause (and one that will itself likely remain a matter of debate).

Along with saying that wisdom begins with the fear of the Lord, the book of Proverbs gives another hint as to how wisdom can be obtained. Proverbs 1:2 and 1:9 suggest that wisdom can be obtained from directive or disciplined instruction by teachers.[10] Perhaps an example of this pedagogical method is embedded in the very structure of Proverbs. The book contains the following sections: introductory poems (Proverbs 1-9), proverbs associated with Solomon (10:1-22:16), the "Words of the Wise" (22:17-24:34), proverbs attributed to Hezekiah (25-29), the "Words of Agur" (30), and finally the "Words of King Lemuel" (31:1-9). Each section builds on and complicates earlier sections, if William P. Brown is correct in his analysis.[11]

If the pedagogy of wisdom follows the pattern of Proverbs, the teaching of wisdom begins with a series of pithy sayings that describe an orderly, just world in which piety or intelligence is rewarded. An example of this viewpoint can be found in Proverbs 12:2: "A good man earns the favor of the Lord, a man of intrigues, His condemnation." These insights, at this point in the book, can largely be gleaned by simple observation of the patterns of life around us. Later sayings revisit the same theme from different angles, thus deepening one's understanding of it by asking the student to synthesize divergent viewpoints. In "the Words of the Wise," theological considerations are added to the mix, as YHWH is named more explicitly and regularly. The focus then moves from relatively simple arenas to complex social problems, as is found in the proverbs associated with Hezekiah, which suggest that even the king can be fallible, neighbors greedy, and the righteous poor. The movement outward to ever more inclusive wholes continues with a focus on the wider non-human creation, as in "the Words of Agur." Finally, the teachers turn, in "the words of King Lemuel," to the task of determining how to rule in such an unruly world. To sum up, the pedagogy of wisdom embodied in Proverbs moves from binary thinking to a more complex understanding of ever more extensive realms before applying the results to a specific context—in this case, the monarchy.

This account of the pedagogy of Proverbs misses, however, an explicit sense of the end game or goal for *chochmah*. So now we return to the question of whether there is, in ancient Hebrew wisdom, an analog to Aristotle's *eudaimonia*. I propose that there is: *shalom*. This term is usually translated as peace, which gives the impression of quiet and lack of conflict. The term is best understood, however, as the integration of the parts into a smoothly functioning whole that does what it was designed to do. Years ago, Lexus advertised its cars by placing crystal goblets all over the hood, roof, and trunk of a car. The car was running and the wheels turning (on rollers so the car didn't actually move across the studio), and not a single glass was broken.[12] This is a vivid image of the Hebrew notion of *shalom*.

A poetic depiction of *shalom* can be found in the TNK in the creation story of Genesis 1:1-2:4a. Probably composed around the time of the Exile, this story begins with God contemplating a watery chaos.[13] From it, God creates an ordered cosmos, first speaking light into being, then moving through six days which climax with the creation of human beings as God's likeness. Surveying all that God has made, God then declares it "very good," and rests. The end here is the opposite of the beginning. Whereas at the beginning of the story we find undifferentiated, indeterminate mess, at the conclusion we find a well-thought-out whole in which the parts add up to something magnificent, a whole in which humans have an important role to play. The parts operate in harmony with one another. All living things—plants, animals, and people—live in symbiotic, peaceful relationships with one another, an image recaptured in the vision of the peaceable kingdom found in Isaiah 11:1-10 and depicted many times by American artist William Hicks.[14] All the pieces fit together as they are supposed to: call it *shalom, eudaimonia, peace, flourishing*. I propose that we consider *shalom*, as described in the Priestly creation story, as the goal toward which wisdom strives and the good that it seeks to achieve, in however partial a form.

So far, we have examined the call of Lady Wisdom in Proverbs, which led to an exploration of the nature of the Hebrew *chokmah*, which required us to engage affinities with ancient Greek ideas of *sophia, techne*, and *phronesis*. The discussion raised three additional topics: how we can develop wisdom, whether Hebrew thought has an equivalent to the Greek *eudaimonia*, and whether wisdom has room for laws and principles. We have addressed the first two issues on the basis of texts found in the TNK. To take up the last, we must move beyond the TNK to ancient Jewish writings that are part of the Apocrypha, texts written by and for Jewish audiences that did not make it into the TNK.

Insights from Beyond the TNK

We have seen that the TNK opens in Genesis 1 with a vision of an orderly, created universe—of *shalom*—an order that seems to be more wishful thinking than fact as the narrative proceeds in Genesis 2. That order is severely called into question by the end of the TNK, with the debates embedded in the Writings, debates that occur when hope for a unified and restored independent nation of Israel seems unlikely. We have seen, in the canonical book of Job, how wisdom has taken a subversive turn. (The same is true of the book of Ecclesiastes.) Perhaps to counter the pessimism of this late wisdom literature (and/or the heated debates preserved in the Writings), non-canonical writers, working at roughly the same time as some of the canonical writers, begin to associate wisdom with the love, contemplation, and interpretation of the Law.[15]

The book Ecclesiasticus (or Sirach), now printed as part of the Apocrypha, is the first place we see this equation of Law and Wisdom. Yeshua ben Sira (Jesus son of Sira), writing during the Greek occupation of ancient Israel, suggests that "whoever holds to the Law will obtain wisdom" (15:1). He goes on to affirm, echoing Proverbs, that "the whole of wisdom is the fear of the Lord," and then adds the claim that "in all wisdom there is fulfillment of the Law" (19:20).[16] In Chapter 24, in a manner again reminiscent of Proverbs, ben Sira personifies wisdom as a prophetess and hostess. Lady Wisdom tells of her role in creation and invites listeners to eat of her provisions so that they will hunger and thirst no more. Then she adds, "All this is the book of the covenant of the Most High God, the Law that Moses commanded us" (24:23). Wisdom thus becomes associated with Law, an association that is suggestive for our purposes.

While scholars debate exactly what ben Sira and others intended to accomplish by equating Law and wisdom, I am not going to enter into those debates. Instead, I want to improvise on this move to answer the question of whether wisdom has a place for rules and principles. The insight I glean from the equation of wisdom with law is that wisdom is necessary for interpreting and applying laws (and, by extension, principles) to specific situations so as to achieve as much *shalom* as is possible in that circumstance. Wisdom would seem to entail the ability to discern the challenges we face when using rules and principles to determine what to do.

There are two primary challenges to such efforts, the first of which is that neither rules nor principles are self-interpreting. We saw this in Chapter Two in our discussion of Adam, Eve, and the Serpent. The "rule" says, "Don't eat under penalty of death," but the rule does not tell us what death means. Does it mean the cessation of biological functioning? This is presumably what it means to Eve. Does it mean a spiritual death? This is the way most Christian commentators understand it. Or does it mean death to a creaturely existence and new life like that of a god? This is what the Serpent suggests. There are multiple possibilities. How do we decide between them? The same is true of principles. What does justice mean? For some, it means fairness—that equal situations require equal treatment. For others, it means that preferential treatment is needed to overcome past inequities. Which understanding of justice do we use?

The second challenge is that conflicting rules and principles might both apply to the same situation. Take a familiar example from the practice of medicine. One of the chief principles of medical ethics is to do no harm (the principle of non-maleficence). Another is to do the patient's good (the principle of beneficence). Yet surgeons, to do what is good for the patient—for example, to remove a tumor—have to harm the body by cutting into it. How do we negotiate between conflicting principles? In this case, we typically justify surgery by some kind of cost-benefit analysis. If the benefits of removing the tumor outweigh the risks of surgery, we consent to the operation. But even then, there may be times when those discriminations are themselves unclear. Is there a rule or principle that guides us then?

The search for rules and/or principles that help us interpret and apply other rules and principles threatens to send us down the proverbial rabbit hole so that we get caught up in an infinite regress of rules or principles. This situation is ultimately untenable, as we cannot, in advance, specify how a rule or principle applies to a specific case. Does this mean that rules and principles have no use in the moral life? No, but it does mean that they are best treated as rules of thumb, a kind of moral shorthand for actions and attitudes that point us to *shalom*, actions and attitudes that we should heed, all things being equal. But when all things are *not* equal, we need wisdom to help us find our way forward.

The Moral Story of the TNK Revisited

As pollsters and psychologists know, the questions we ask influence the answers we get. Readers of the Bible should acknowledge this fact, as well. In this book, I have invited readers to engage in a novel thought experiment that (1) reads the Old Testament as Hebrew Bible, (2) assumes that, despite the diverse historical and authorial origins of these texts, they can be read as telling a continuous story, (3) is about moral development. In doing so, we discover that the Hebrew Bible's story of moral development culminates with a call to develop wisdom in the midst of conflicting voices that debate what is good, true, and right.

In this story, making rules and principles the center of morality does not provide a stable basis for morality. People will sometimes break the rules and principles that they know and acknowledge as valid. People also have to apply laws and hence discover that others may differ in interpretation and application of those laws. Principles, too, must be interpreted. Moreover, given their abstract nature, how to apply principles to concrete situations becomes even more difficult than more specific laws. A healthy moral life thus is forced to move beyond adherence to social conventions (Law) or post-conventional appeal to principles (Prophets). A healthy moral life requires the development of the virtue of wisdom, which begins with a move away from self-centeredness and the desire for always clear-cut, right and wrong answers to the challenges we face. Wisdom entails having a vision of the good that serves as a goal for our actions and becoming increasingly skilled in perceiving the relevant details of the complex, thickly textured questions and problems we often face.

This happens first under the guidance of teachers who encourage us to reflect carefully and faithfully. This is something that I have tried to do in this book: to point out some of the interesting and sometimes vexing diversity that can be found in the TNK and to invite us to reflect critically and faithfully on that diversity. My hope is that this experiment has moved us further down the path toward wisdom so that we, like the ancient Israelites, can learn better how to negotiate, as God's people, a complex and ambiguous world full of competing advice on what is good, right, true, and beautiful.

Exercises in Discernment

If wisdom is learned by discerning details and complexities in the face of disagreement so that we can attain the most of the good possible in the circumstance, then we cannot leave this book without engaging in some practice exercises in discernment. What follows are some topics that ask us to wrestle with some of the diversity within the TNK, not all of which is explicitly moral in nature. Still, learning to see and wrestle with the details is a key skill in practical wisdom, and so practice in other domains may help us develop this component of wisdom.

1. *Consider diverse accounts of Creation.* The Torah contains two radically different accounts of how the universe began: the Priestly account, as told in Genesis 1:1-2:4a, and the Yahwistic account, told in Genesis 2:4b-25. Compare the two accounts by completing the following chart:

	Genesis 1:1-2:4a	Genesis 2:4b-25
What is the setting of the story?		
What is created first?		
What is created last?		
What terms are used to describe human beings?		
What are human beings commanded to do?		
What limits are placed on human beings?		

- What are the most striking differences?

- What are the most striking similarities?

- What options do you see for addressing how the stories are not the same?

- What do you think is the wisest way to do so? Why?

2. *Consider diverse perspectives on God.* We have seen at several points in the TNK that authors sometimes characterize God in unflattering ways. Earlier in this work, I have called particular attention to some of the less palatable characterizations: the temperamental God of Genesis 3, the God who has to be cajoled into doing the right things in the laments, and the fiendish God of Job. But there are, of course, more positive views to be found in the TNK.

Look again at the two creation stories and complete this chart about how God is described.

	Genesis 1:1-2:4a	Genesis 2:4b-25
Does God seem to know what God is doing? Explain.		
Where does God "stand" in relation to creation: close up or far away?		
By what means does God create? How powerful does God seem to be?		

Just a few of the other ways that God is portrayed in the TNK include warrior (in Exodus, where God battles the Egyptians on behalf of the Israelites), all-condemning judge (Amos), and scorned husband (Hosea). Now consider one more: God in Daniel 7:9. Jack Miles notes that this is the last time God shows up as a character in the TNK, now called "the Ancient of Days." The text describes God in part by saying that "the hair of His head was like lamb's wool," i.e., white. The point of the symbolism seems to be to highlight God's age and the wisdom that comes with age. Look further into these texts and discuss the following questions:

- What options do you see for addressing how different authors depict God in very different ways?

- Given the final depiction of God in Daniel, is it fair to say that God becomes wise over the course of the events depicted in the TNK?

- What is the wisest way to understand these different views of God? Explain.

3. *Consider diverse teachings on sex and marriage.* Genesis 2:21-25 tells the story of Eve's creation and ends with what appears to be a model of lifelong, monogamous, heterosexual marriage. On the other hand, Genesis 16:1-4 contains part of the story of Abraham impregnating Hagar, his wife's servant, to produce a male heir, a story told with no overt disapproval of his actions. Deuteronomy 24:1-4 makes provision for divorce, which would seem to undo Genesis 2. Deuteronomy 25:5-10 commands the practice of Levirite marriage so that the brother of a man who dies without children should sire children with his sister-in-law, a practice that would both allow for the line to continue and protect the widow. Song of Songs is a book of erotic poetry that celebrates the sexual exploits of two lovers, who may or may not be married. Look further into these texts and discuss the following questions:

- What options do you see for addressing these facts about different messages found in the TNK about sex and marriage?

- What is the wisest way to understand these different views? Why?

4. *Consider the overall problem of biblical diversity.* There are two easy ways to deal with biblical diversity. The first is to deny the diversity and explain it away by imposing on the text our preexisting ideas about God and morality. The other is to think about the texts in their historical contexts only. We could thus say that each book represents the attempt of a particular author at a particular time to address a need or problem for a particular audience—and so whether a particular view is right or not depends on the context. Discuss the following questions:

- What do you see as the strengths and weaknesses of each option?

- Do you see any other options? What are their strengths and weaknesses?

- What do you think is the wisest way of dealing with these differences? Why?

5. Take one of the moral issues we have mentioned in this chapter: sex and marriage, treatment of foreigners, response to enemies (or pick another). What can we learn from these ancient texts about what a wise response to our contemporary debates might be?

Endnotes

[1]For more on Lady Wisdom, see Leo G. Perdue, *Wisdom Literature: A Theological History* (Louisville: Westminster John Knox Press, 2007), 52ff.; Roland E. Murphy, *The Tree of Life: An Exploration of Biblical Wisdom Literature* (Grand Rapids: William B. Eerdmans, 1990), 135ff.; and Jack Miles, *God: A Biography* (New York: Vintage Books, 1995), 290-297.

[2]See James Crenshaw, *Old Testament Wisdom: An Introduction*, Revised and Enlarged (Louisville: Westminster John Knox, 1998), 44-45; Donn F. Morgan, *The Making of Sages: Biblical Wisdom and Contemporary Culture* (Harrisburg, PA: Trinity Press, 2002), 19-21; and Murphy, 3-5.

[3]Douglas A. Knight and Amy-Jill Levine, *The Meaning of the Bible* (New York: HarperOne, 2011), 428.

[4]William P. Brown, *Wisdom's Wonder: Character, Creation, and Crisis in the Bible's Wisdom Literature* (Grand Rapids: William B. Eerdmans, 2014), 36.

[5]Paul S. Fiddes, *Seeing the World and Knowing God: Hebrew Wisdom and Christian Doctrine in a Late-Modern Context* (New York: Oxford University Press, 2013), 6-8.

[6]Fiddes, 9-10.

[7]Aristotle discusses practical wisdom in Book VI of *Nicomachean Ethics.*

[8]I find intriguing the sequence of the books that make up the Writings. Proverbs is preceded in the canon by Psalms, the hymnbook of worship in the second Temple. Could it be that the sequence of Psalms and Proverbs symbolically embodies the claim that wisdom begins with the fear (worship) of God?

[9]See Brown, *Wisdom's Wonder*, 37ff. This notion of fear may originally have referred more narrowly to what happens when one fails to fulfill one's covenantal obligations (see Crenshaw, 79).

[10]Morgan compares the method of instruction to contemporary pedagogies, such as that of reflective practice (see Morgan 38-39 and 161-162). This pedagogy therefore resonates with Aristotle's account of moral development.

[11]Here I draw from both Brown, *Wisdom's Wonder* 36 and his "The Pedagogy of Proverbs 10:1-31:9," in *Character and Scripture: Moral Formation, Community, and Biblical Interpretation*, edited by William P. Brown (Grand Rapids: William B. Eerdmans Publishing Company, 2002), 150-182.

[12]You can watch the commercial at https://www.youtube.com/watch?v=X1vZen BX4-0 (accessed 11 February 2017).

[13]Scholars attribute this creation story to the Priestly source. Read in its canonical place, it therefore sets up a series of expectations that do not pan out in the rest of the narrative, for as we move into the rest of the Law—beginning with the second, or Yahwistic, creation story that we discussed in Chapter Two—we find that all of the pieces do not, in reality, fit together harmoniously. Life does not go smoothly. People and God seem to act all too often with reckless abandon. For more on the similarities and differences between the two stories, see the exercises in discernment at the end

of this chapter.

[14]The Christian New Testament uses different symbolism to make a compatible point in the climactic vision of the heavenly city in Revelation 20-22. There, all that opposes God is excluded from creation and God is present directly to all peoples, who have ready access not only to the "river of life" but also to the fruit of the "tree of life," which in Genesis 3 was a possibility foreclosed to Adam and Eve. In short, all of creation exists in glorious harmony.

[15]See Murphy, 76; Knight and Levine, 434; and Fiddes, 19.

[16]Miles suggests one way that we might understand how wisdom fulfills the law is that "wisdom broadens and heightens Torah by discussing character formation and prudence, about which Torah is silent" (293).

APPENDIX

Moral Development and Wisdom in Contemporary Psychology

I am convinced that people of faith can learn something valuable about moral development from reading the TNK in the way we have done here. One way to discover that value is to put it into conversation with recent psychology. As noted in the preface, much moral psychology has been influenced by Lawrence Kohlberg's account of moral reasoning. To recap, Kohlberg identifies six stages in the development of moral reasoning clustered into three levels that he calls the pre-conventional, conventional and post-conventional. In pre-conventional reasoning, moral decisions are based on the impact they will have on the self. In conventional moral reasoning, decisions are based on social conventions—that is, what other people, customs, laws, etc., expect of us. People who reason at the post-conventional level base their decisions on so-called "transcendent ideals," such as human rights or justice.

To determine the stage at which one reasons, Kohlberg asks students to consider several dilemmas and then describe what they would do and explain why. One of the best known of these scenarios is the Heinz dilemma. To summarize: Heinz's wife is sick with a serious illness. There is a medicine that can cure the disease, but it is expensive and Heinz does not have enough money for it or a way to raise enough money in time. Despite the dire situation, the druggist refuses to give the medicine to Heinz. What should Heinz do—should he let his wife die, or should he break into the pharmacy and steal the drug?

In the preface, I mentioned briefly that Kohlberg's work has been criticized on a number of fronts. For example, some studies found that few people attained post-conventional levels of moral reasoning, thus leading

Try it Out

In the space below, reflect on what you would do if you were Heinz, and why.

Where do your reasons fall in Kohlberg's schema? Are you more concerned about what will happen to Heinz if he gets caught? Are you more concerned with breaking the law? Are you more concerned with preserving human life?

Of course, one scenario is not sufficient to determine where you fall, but this one exercise can hint at what your "default" stage of moral reasoning might be.

Kohlberg at one point to doubt the existence of Stage 6. Other studies found that those who exhibit Stage 5 reasoning have participated in graduate education, while those who have attained Stage 6 have all received formal training in philosophy.[1] Moreover, Kohlberg and others realized fairly quickly that people who exhibit high levels of moral reasoning do not always *act* morally. Put differently, there is often a disconnect between behavior and stage of reasoning.[2]

This disconnect led James Rest to develop a four-component model of morality. According to Rest, there are four interdependent psychological processes that must connect for one's behavior to accord with one's reasoning.[3] The first is that of interpretation. Persons must be able to "read" the moral import of a situation and sort through various plans of action and their consequences. Secondly, persons must be willing and able to judge a course of action as morally right or obligatory. Thirdly, one must prioritize moral values over other concerns. Finally, the agent must have both a strong enough self-identity and the requisite skills by which to implement action.

Darcia Narvaez, a psychologist at the University of Notre Dame and student of Rest, refines and expands this model. She compares the development of character to the development of expertise.[4] At one level is ethical sensitivity—the ability to perceive clues from the environment, including the emotional expressions and perspectives of others, as well as to perceive possible actions and their consequences. Another level is that of ethical judgment that moves beyond initial perceptions to skillful reasoning about what action is most ethical in the circumstances. A third level is what Narvaez calls ethical focus, or the ability to prioritize moral considerations over others. A final level is that of action, i.e., implementing the plans made in spite of any difficulties one encounters.

Since the time of Kohlberg and Rest, it is generally conceded that moral psychology has moved into a post-Kohlberg phase, but it is not entirely clear what the future of moral psychology might be. I suspect that wisdom might fruitfully define the next phase. While Rest and Narvaez are usually described as still fitting into the Kohlberg model, I think they point beyond it toward wisdom. To be sure, they do not explicitly refer to wisdom, but the idea is there tacitly: they talk about the kinds of moves one must make to put knowledge to use in service of the good.[5] What is tacit in their work becomes more explicit in that of the psychologists who study wisdom.

Paul Baltes and Ursula Staudinger at the Max Planck Institute for Human Development in Berlin define wisdom as expertise in "the fundamental pragmatics of life," such as conduct and the construction of meaning for life in various contexts: education, family, work, friends, and the common good.[6] Developing this expertise requires engaging an open and ill-defined body of knowledge, wrestling with the differences in values held by different people, and managing uncertainty. In doing so, people must integrate factual knowledge ("what") with procedural knowledge ("how"). Robert J. Sternberg says even more explicitly that this integration must serve the common good. Doing so requires achieving a complex balance at two main levels, the human and the environmental. At the human level, wisdom requires balancing intrapersonal, interpersonal, and extrapersonal interests. At the environmental level, those human interests have to be directed to a course of action that best balances the options of adapting to existing environments, modifying those environments, or moving to new environments. Sternberg thus identifies six components to wisdom: knowledge, discernment, a judicial thinking style that probes beneath surface appearances to discover how and why things happen as they do, tolerance of ambiguity, motivation to understand, and appreciation for the limits and possibilities of action in a specific context.[7]

Putting all this together, I think we can arrive at a model for ethical reflection and action that looks something like the illustration on the following page.

The model highlights a recursive practice that involves perceiving something is out of synch morally, exploring the details of the situation, deciding on a course of action, acting, and then learning from that action and its results for the next time. With practice over time, we develop wisdom, a kind of expertise that connects the dots between content knowledge and process knowledge, expertise that makes the wise person seem to work effortlessly.[8]

One way to practice these skills can be found in Sternberg's work, a method that has informed this book and my teaching of the TNK as an

Morality
(experience of
conflicting goods)

Ethics
(reflection on the experience)

Three questions: Who are we? What's going on? What ought we to do?

Three tasks: analytical, normative, and formative

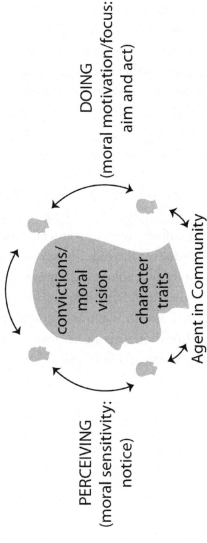

EXPLORING
(moral judgment and motivation: think and aim)

DOING
(moral motivation/focus:
aim and act)

convictions/
moral
vision

character
traits

Agent in Community

PERCEIVING
(moral sensitivity:
notice)

EVALUATING
(moral judgment and motivation: think and aim)

invitation to develop wisdom.[9] Sternberg has developed ways of teaching wisdom in the classroom that begin with having students read classic works in the context of history so that students do not judge characters solely by contemporary standards. They thereby develop an ability to think "dialogically," from the perspective of others, and "dialectically," to see how questions and answers change over time. Besides reading classic texts, students discuss and write about the insights they have gleaned from these works, especially about how to apply those insights to their own lives and social settings. In doing so, instructors encourage students both to reflect on the ends to which these insights might be put and whether those are good ends, or ends that benefit not only self but others.

My point here is not to overwhelm readers with details of divergent yet largely compatible—or at least intersecting—accounts of moral development and wisdom.[10] Instead, I mean to suggest two things. The first is that contemporary psychology may prove to be a useful ally in the quest for wisdom by people of faith. The second is that, if there is any merit in reading the TNK as an invitation to develop wisdom, then psychology might benefit from intensifying its investigations into wisdom, perhaps finding in the ancient notion of *chockmah* a way of defining and measuring wisdom.

Endnotes

[1] See Lynn Swaner, "Educating for Personal and Social Responsibility: A Planning Project of the Association of American Colleges and Universities" (2004), 9.

[2] See also Elizabeth C. Vozzola, *Moral Development: Theory and Applications* (New York and London: Routledge, 2014), 32-33. Chapter 4 explores in greater depth the challenges to these cognitive developmental theories.

[3] James Rest with Muriel Bebeau and Joseph Volker, "An Overview of the Psychology of Morality" in *Moral Development: Advances in Research and Theory* (New York: Praeger, 1986), 3-18.

[4] This description draws from her "Integrative Ethical Education" in *Handbook of Moral Development*, Melanie Killen and Judith G. Smetana, eds. (Mahwah, NJ: Lawrence Erblaum Associates, 2006), 717, as well as her "The Neo-Kohlbergian Tradition and Beyond: Schemas, Expertise, and Character" in *Moral Motivation Through the Lifespan*, Gustavo Carlo and Carolyn Pope Edwards, eds. (Lincoln, NE: University of Nebraska Press, 2005), 138-148.

[5] In her later work, Narvaez has begun to talk about wisdom explicitly. See, for example, pp. 230-298 in her *Neurobiology and the Development of Human Morality: Evolution, Culture and Wisdom* (New York: W.W. Norton and Company), 2014.

[6] See Paul B. Baltes and Ursula M. Staudinger, "Wisdom: a Metaheuristic (Pragmatic) to Orchestrate Mind and Virtue Toward Excellence." *American Psychologist* 55:1 (January 2000):12-136.

[7] My summary draws on Robert J. Sternberg, "A Balance Theory of Wisdom." *Review of General Psychology* 2:4 (1998):347-365.

[8] The work on wisdom needs to engage more closely the work on automaticity and heuristics—the fact that many of our decisions seem to be made quickly, even automatically, without conscious deliberation. For examples of work in this area, see the suggestions for further reading.

[9] This summary draws from Robert J. Sternberg, "Why Schools Should Teach for Wisdom: The Balance Theory of Wisdom in Educational Settings." *Educational Psychologist* 36 (4): 238-239.

[10] I have hinted at some of the intersections in my "In Defence of Aristotle on Character: Toward a Synthesis of Recent Psychology, Neuroscience, and the Thought of Michael Polanyi." *Journal of Moral Education* 41, no. 2 (2012): 155-170.

For Further Reading

Standard Textbook Introductions to the Old Testament

- Barry Bandstra. *Reading the Old Testament*. 3rd edition. Belmont, CA: Thomson/Wadsworth, 2004.

- Michael D. Coogan. *A Brief Introduction to the Old Testament: The Hebrew Bible in Its Context*. New York: Oxford University Press, 2009.

- Stephen L. Harris and Robert L. Platzner. *The Old Testament: An Introduction to the Hebrew Bible*. 2nd edition. New York: McGraw-Hill, 2008.

On the Literary Interpretation of the Bible

- Robert Alter. *The Art of Biblical Narrative*. New York: Basic Books, 1981.

On Canonical Criticism

- Brevard Childs. *Introduction to the Old Testament as Scripture*. Philadelphia: Fortress Press, 1979.

On Israelite Prophecy

- Walter Brueggemann. *The Prophetic Imagination*. 2nd edition. Minneapolis: Augsburg Fortress, 2001.

- Victor H. Matthews. *The Social World of the Hebrew Prophets*. Peabody, MA: Hendrickson Publishers, Inc., 2001.

- Gerhardt von Rad. *The Message of the Prophets*. Trans. D.M.G. Stalker. London: SCM Press, LTD., 1968.

On the Greek Period and Maccabean Revolt

- John Bright. *A History of Ancient Israel.* 4th edition, with an introduction and appendix by William P. Brown. Louisville: Westminster John Knox, 2000. Chapters 10-12.

On Job

- Samuel E. Ballentine. *Have You Considered My Servant, Job? Understanding the Biblical Archetype of Patience.* Columbia, SC: University of South Carolina Press, 2015.

- Carol Newsom. *The Book of Job: A Contest of Moral Imaginations.* New York: Oxford University Press, 2003.

On Aristotle

- Kristjan Kristjansson. *Aristotle, Emotions, and Education.* Burlington, VT: Ashgate Publishing Co., 2007.

- Daniel C. Russell. *Practical Intelligence and the Virtues.* New York: Oxford University Press), 2009.

- Nancy Sherman. *The Fabric of Character.* New York: Oxford University Press, 1989.

On Practical Wisdom

- Mark Jones. "Practical Wisdom and Vocation in Professional Formation," pp. 193-198 in *Toward Human Flourishing: Character, Practical Wisdom, and Professional Formation,* edited by Mark Jones, Paul Lewis, and Kellly Reffitt. Macon, GA: Mercer University Press, 2013.

- Barry Schwartz and Kenneth Sharpe. *Practical Wisdom: The Right Way to Do the Right Thing.* New York: Riverhead Books, 2010.

On Moral Psychology after Kohlberg

- See the entire issue of the *Journal of Moral Education*, September 2009 (Vol. 38, No. 3).

- Richard A. Dienstbier, Gustavo Carlo, and Carolyn Pope Edwards, editors, *Moral Motivation through the Life Span*. Volume 51 of the Nebraska Symposium on Motivation. Lincoln, NE: University of Nebraska Press, 2005.

- Kristjan Kristjansson. *The Self and Its Emotions*. New York: Cambridge University Press, 2010.

- Elizabeth C. Vozzola, *Moral Development: Theory and Applications*. New York and London: Routledge, 2014.

On Automaticity and Intuitions

- Malcolm Gladwell. *Blink: The Power of Thinking Without Thinking*. New York: Back Bay Books, 2005.

- Daniel Kahneman. *Thinking Fast and Slow*. New York: Farrar, Straus and Giroux, 2011.

- Robin M. Hogarth. *Educating Intuition*. Chicago: University of Chicago Press, 2001.

- Gerd Gigerenzer. *Gut Feelings: The Intelligence of the Unconscious*. New York: Penguin, 2007.

Bibliography

Aristotle. *Nichomachean Ethics.* Trans. Martin Ostwald. The Library of Liberal Arts. New York: Macmillan Publishing Company, 1986.

Baltes, Paul B. and Ursula M. Staudinger. "Wisdom: a Metaheuristic (Pragmatic) to Orchestrate Mind and Virtue Toward Excellence." *American Psychologist* 55, no. 1 (2000):122-136.

Blumenthal, David R. *Facing the Abusing God.* Louisville: Westminster John Knox, 1993.

Borg, Marcus. *Reading the Bible Again for the First Time.* New York: HarperCollins, 2001.

Brown, William P. "The Pedagogy of Proverbs 10:1-31:9," in *Character and Scripture: Moral Formation, Community, and Biblical Interpretation,* edited by William P. Brown, 150-182. Grand Rapids: William. B. Eerdmans Publishing Company, 2002.

_____. *Wisdom's Wonder: Character, Creation, and Crisis in the Bible's Wisdom Literature.* Grand Rapids, MI: William B. Eerdmans Publishing Co., 2014.

Crenshaw, James. *Old Testament Wisdom: An Introduction.* Revised and Enlarged edition. Louisville: Westminster John Knox, 1998.

Fiddes, Paul S. *Seeing the World and Knowing God: Hebrew Wisdom and Christian Doctrine in a Late-Modern Context.* New York: Oxford University Press, 2013.

Garver, Eugene. *For the Sake of Argument: Practical Reasoning, Character, and the Ethics of Belief.* Chicago: University of Chicago Press, 2004.

Knight, Douglas A. and Amy-Jill Levine. *The Meaning of the Bible.* New York: HarperOne, 2011.

Lewis, Paul. "In Defence of Aristotle on Character: Toward a Synthesis of Recent Psychology, Neuroscience, and the Thought of Michael

Polanyi." *Journal of Moral Education* 41, no. 2 (2012): 155-170.

May, James Luther. *Amos,* The Old Testament Library. Philadelphia: The Westminster Press, 1969.

Miles, Jack. God: *A Biography.* New York: Vintage Books, 1995.

Morgan, Donn F. *The Making of Sages: Biblical Wisdom and Contemporary Culture.* Harrisburg, PA: Trinity Press, 2002.

Murphy, Roland E. *The Tree of Life: An Exploration of Biblical Wisdom Literature.* Grand Rapids: William B. Eerdmans, 1990.

Narvaez, Darcia. "Integrative Ethical Education." In *Handbook of Moral Development,* edited by Melanie Killen and Judith G. Smetana, 703-734. Mahwah, NJ: Lawrence Erblaum Associates, 2006.

_____. "The Neo-Kohlbergian Tradition and Beyond: Schemas, Expertise, and Character." In *Moral Motivation Through the Lifespan,* edited by Gustavo Carlo and Carolyn Pope Edwards, 119-163. Lincoln, NE: University of Nebraska Press, 2005.

_____. *Neurobiology and the Development of Human Morality: Evolution, Culture and Wisdom.* New York: W.W. Norton and Company, 2014.

Perdue, Leo G. *Wisdom Literature: A Theological History.* Louisville: Westminster John Knox Press, 2007.

Rest, James with Muriel Bebeau and Joseph Volker. "An Overview of the Psychology of Morality." In *Moral Development: Advances in Research and Theory,* edited by James Rest, 1-27. New York: Praeger, 1986.

Rohr, Richard. *Falling Upward: A Spirituality for the Two Halves of Life.* San Francisco: Josey-Bass, 2011.

Sternberg, Robert J. "A Balance Theory of Wisdom." *Review of General Psychology* 2:4 (1998): 347-365.

_____. "Why Schools Should Teach for Wisdom: The Balance Theory of Wisdom in Educational Settings." *Educational Psychologist* 36, 4 (2001): 227-245.

Surin, Kenneth. *Theology and the Problem of Evil.* New York: Basil Blackwell, Inc., 1986.

Swaner, Lynn. "Educating for Personal and Social Responsibility: A Planning Project of the Association of American Colleges and Universities," 2004.

Vozzola, Elizabeth C. *Moral Development: Theory and Applications.* New York and London: Routledge, 2014.

Wiesel, Elie. "Judaism: The Chosen People." *The Long Search.* By Ronald Eyre. Ambrose Video: 1977.

CPSIA information can be obtained
at www.ICGtesting.com
Printed in the USA
LVOW13s1426280617
539681LV00014B/1233/P